When I Was in New York

GARY ZARR

authorHOUSE®

AuthorHouse™
1663 Liberty Drive
Bloomington, IN 47403
www.authorhouse.com
Phone: 1-800-839-8640

Cover: What is it about the clouds? Gary Zarr

*This book is set in Bodoni, a series of serif typefaces
first designed by Giambattista Bodoni (1740-1813) in 1798.*

First published by AuthorHouse   12/01/2011

ISBN: 978-1-4670-3744-0 (sc)
ISBN: 978-1-4670-3745-7 (hc)
ISBN: 978-1-4670-3746-4 (ebk)

Library of Congress Control Number: 2011916513

Printed in the United States of America

This book is printed on acid-free paper.

for Danny and Emily
spirited wings who helped me fly again

Joey, Wayne, Cliff and Tesla helped me make this book.
Richie reminded me one night. Russ and Laura shared
paradise with me when I desperately needed it.

Desire Paths

Desire Paths

In a noisy new bar
when you recited
Loving-kindness Meditation
you spoke the line,
"May I be well,"
and you wept silently, gently.
Then the downpour cleansed us
as we ran as fast as we could
laughing to get safely home.

Disease

disease is
being alive
in mysterious ways
that spin
beyond
our control
knowing
past where we can
ever be

Maples

From the porch I watch
two immense maples
side by side,
one green, full
waving in the late
summer sun.
The other broken,
skeletal
just about dead in the
evening breeze.
Two maples rustle.
The longer I gaze
the more they look the
same.

Sleepless

Nightingale and me
sleepless tonight.
The cat purrs on the pillow,
the world vibrates darkness.
Outside freezing, clear.
Restless inside
lit with a single candle,
a laptop screen, dreams.

Porch Moon

I watch the moon pass
between two dark trees
in the cold
with her
on the porch.
It dawns on me again
that we are meant to be parted.
As we love
we are each taken away.

Tulips

Even if you stared
forever
you wouldn't
be
able
to see
the flaming red tulips
with yellow and black streaks inside
silently swoop, sway
slow motion
like drooping graceful swans
inevitably
pulled
earthward.

The Call

I'll see you
in a little bit.
My phone's
about to die.

Gary Zarr

Night

I wanted night to go
where I couldn't see it anymore
feel it anymore.
I wanted darkness to vanish
like an unseen ocean
in breezes blowing from God knows where.
The paperback on the small plastic table
silently flips open, closes.
Alone with a few wayward, lost stars,
I wonder if there is an end to pain.
I see that your death will arrive
quietly in flurries
barely discernable flakes of doom
a storm that buries us with sleepy white cat paws
imperceptibly tickling our faces
till the drifts pile too high
for us to breathe or kiss any more.
No one will ever hear us sing, our final cries.
Our way of playing with this pulsing world will cease
and every single thing will simply stop for you and me.
There will be no hope of melting the unyielding walls of icy snow
which silently bury our fiery world.
And even my last burning tears of defiance
will freeze to stone in my wide-open, starry yearning eyes.

Harmony

and it was all
I was able to see
this devastating scene
unfolds
my everlasting
stormy harmony

New England Getaway

Nothing must be left unsaid my love
not now, not at this sacred time
not when monsters obscure the sun
and dark birds screech over cornfields
and frightened kids are yanked down streets
into sealed rooms where they don't want to go.
We must hold each other's hands tight,
walk this serious path
yet still play around with joy
determined to mine each moment
to learn, to love, content.
You said, "I'm going to have wine for dinner, Gar,
even though I said I wouldn't."
And then, "I don't think we'll come back again
because we've done everything we can here."
I knew you were right
as I turned the air conditioner up a notch
and dressed for dinner while you showered.
I hid under the covers in the pale yellow room,
thought about the mountains
and the lakes we passed that morning.
Even though you usually played navigator
you offered to drive because you said I looked tired.
We never did find the magic country road from last year
but instead drove a new one with wild flowers,
square brick buildings by running rivers,
shivering ponds with bobbing flowers and egrets.
My legs warmed in bed, I heard the shower stop.
I knew you were toweling your body dry.
Yesterday you showed me the scar on your belly.
You wanted me to feel the knotted cord

beneath your pale skin on the edges of the smiling incision.
The falling sun darkens the greens
in the trees through the blinds.
You emerge from the bathroom shining
in your happy blue flower sun dress.
And as you hum and comb your hair
I wonder where we go from here.

Severe Weather

"It's a snow bomb."
Giant red snowflakes
swirl around my head.
Bitter cold realization.

A severe weather pattern.
Dazed, crash through a battered gray door.
Damp shivering alone.
Huddle on cement steps.

The howling came too fast.
Silent scarlet blizzard
biting direct—inescapable.
Inside finally we understand
"We may not make it out alive."

Ferry Ride

My hands rested on the loose, moving timbers.
The fence, thick as trees, seemed like a pier.
You stood to my right.
We may have held hands.
We're nearing the island, I thought but didn't say,
as the busy, growing town drew close to our ferry,
which stretched as large as a football field,
flat, so wide I couldn't see far enough to find its edges,
filled with hundreds of people, all without faces.
I didn't want to have to leave you.
I didn't want to have to leave you there.
The thud of arrival—we shuddered, and then we docked.
"I don't want this to be! I don't want this to happen!"
I shouted like a child although I didn't make a sound.
I pulled you close, pushed my face into your bomber jacket.
There was salt too, spray from the sea, my tears,
I'm not sure what else.

Half Asleep

Gray winter morning.
Infinite fingers of cold rain
play the air conditioner,
syncopate the window sill
with unpredictable rhythms.
Overhead the wide fan whirs backup.
I'm tumbling silently back asleep.
A bird far off calls.

Coffee

Who knew that our love would
come to rest in the coffee
this morning the sound
of percolating water
bubbling in the kitchen
where the strange potted plant
we gave up for dead
flowers
white in early spring
for the two of us
beaming like small kids.

Christmas Tree

Beautiful tree
sorrowful tree
tree we decorated
and adored so.
Where are you going
shimmering blue and red
green and yellow
colored with such sadness?

For Jackie Boy

Even the funniest
most furious
yield
eventually
give in
like children
after dinner
at dusk
lie down
after the day's adventures
relax
despite themselves
they do
finally
lie down
turn over
rest
and sleep
rest
go somewhere
far away
and that's okay.
It's okay
Jackie Boy.
It's okay
to let yourself
rest.

Gary Zarr

Delirious Love

I understand now
what an immense journey
it can be from this side
of the coffee table
to the other.
Feverish, she sits in her pale blue nightgown
on the edge of the couch
peeling a Clementine,
asks sweetly, "Want some?"
I am with you now my dear
though you don't know
who I am.
Later under the covers,
the year pyrotechnically ending,
your over-heated hand,
moist forehead,
you do
seem
to know
me.
Maybe
you
recognize
me.
You know me.
You know me.

Watch

I raise it now
the significance of this watch
which without my left wrist
warm and flexible
will it end up on a table or a shelf
in a drawer or a box
crammed with other forlorn objects
that do not possess owners.
Today this watch is labeled "mine"
but inevitably, truly,
it belongs to no one at all.
And neither do I really.

Scarcity

Every
thing
must be
considered
in light
of scarcity.

Touch Me

When they come
to touch me
they always wear latex gloves
or else pat me through blankets
so when I felt your naked fingers
under the covers
touch me
my skin reminded me
that I was still a woman.

Christmas Prayer

There's a calmness in the Christmas tree this year
a stillness glitters with the magic of the woods
that quiet, hidden, silent cold place under forest trees
where the snow's dark night blue
where my footfalls pray
for better times
as they sink as far as they can go
to reach the stars.

Underwater Man

Slowly
I let waves
cover me
completely
knowing I can
still
breathe under water
a gift I received
before I was ever born.

Thinning the Herd

The scruffy tan lion crouches in the bush
not far from the nervous, dancing herd of zebra
twitching and drinking beside the gazelles at the pool.
I'm pleased my new TV has such great reception.
The narrator's deep voice explains
how lions hunt with their clumsy cubs playing nearby.
From the rising pitch of the background music
I assume the coiled mass of muscle and bone is about to spring.
The panicked herd gallops away in unison
their legs in time like a Broadway chorus line.
Their eyes bulge at oncoming, racing, snarling death,
as two bombs packed with claws explode into the back of an unlucky zebra.
I turn away unable to watch
this inevitable thinning of the herd,
necessary perhaps in the grand scheme of nature
to balance the planets orbiting along invisible highways.
But not now, not for me, after a couple of beers, alone.
You in the hospital again for an overnight stay.
Instead, I quickly leave the room to take a piss.

On the Bench with Her

"It's so great to be close to the trees," you said,
relieved, drinking in life from the earth to the tops of the branches.
Pure white clouds floated silently east
over the brick apartment buildings lit yellowish
in the autumn afternoon sun with kids laughing in the playground.
Seniors marched past, a young guy in a red jogging suit,
kids ambled absent-mindedly home from school.
"They cut down all the trees; they cut down all the trees,"
an angry business woman said, though we didn't respond.
Your hand was very warm, you didn't speak much.
You seemed intent on gazing at what was outside
in an inner sort of tranquil way.
About the cavalcade of strollers and mothers and nannies,
"Lots of babies," you commented, pulling your hood on.
Also: "It's funny about humanity, everyone has their own story."
after a burly woman playing a harmonica walked stray-dog-like along the Oval.
Later upstairs, you lowered yourself slowly onto the couch.
Puffing, you closed your eyes, exhausted by the short walk
to the bench, which seemed like it was in another part of the world.
My love, I also try to catch my breath from our journey so far way.

Geese

"Did you see the geese?" she asked,
her eyes shining childlike.
They flew overhead to a pond
on a farm down the road
in the afternoon while I took a nap.
They floated and preened in the gray-blue water
shivered in the pond in autumn,
which arrives so often
just before winter.

Last Sunflower

Last
sunflower
of summer
where
are you running
in the rain?
Lightning cracks
cornfields and pastures
crashes over us.
Last
sunflower
of summer
what are you thinking
out there alone
in the rain?
Show me
the secret place
where the sun hides.
Last sunflower
of summer
where
are you running
in the rain?

What's Hidden Beneath the Lawn

In the late afternoon spring sun the expanse of the lawn
we finally finished mowing this morning slouches easy.
Olive green rows of cut grass curve in orderly loops
like a horizontal terrace garden in the Andes.
But only we know that where birds peacefully feed
the huge wooden red barn stood years ago
filled with car parts and broken greasy desks,
crammed with mechanics' tools, cigars
half-empty whiskey bottles,
file cabinets overflowing with musty, canceled checks,
all those Christmas presents you weren't supposed to see yet.
That inside the red barn a huge blower used to thaw our frozen cars
in the dead of winter.
That the upstairs fragile, floor boards creaked
where mysterious chicken coops were long ago.
The thin ancient cement floor, crumbled to fine gravel underfoot,
a cool place out of the summer heat, killer January storms,
a protected spot to have a beer, to try to get an engine running again,
a homely inner world of tinkering and local guys making small talk.
You wouldn't know this part of the lawn is where the barn is buried
and the small pond too, the one he dug when the girls were small.
You wouldn't know except if you gazed at the grass long enough
got lost in each blade, every secret of what used to be
in what's disguised as an immaculately kept lawn
beside a rambling country house.

Burn Barrel

The solitary burn barrel
rusts on the lawn
just beyond the house.
Around its brown corroding bottom
silly milky green weeds
grow hopefully
wave in the summer wind
intertwined with disintegrating metal,
protected by the circular barrel base
from the inexorable
electric mower blades
that are surely coming.

Country Ending

She lays on her back smiling on the grassy hillside
the cat beside her in the summer sun.
Two trees tower over her.
Shadows dance in the soft afternoon breeze.
Sunset is not far off
with its chorus of birds and purple clouds
when a contented country day ends
with a gentle sensual sigh.

Desert Moon

I gaze
at the hazy moon
in the desert
alone
over a truck
racing in the night.

How Love Goes

For Gail

Comerado, I give you my hand!
I give you love more precious than money,
I give you myself before preaching or law;
Will you give me yourself? will you come travel with me?
Shall we stick by each other as long as we live?

Song of the Open Road
Walt Whitman

I Leaving

> *Come gentle hearts have pity on my sighs*
> *As mournful from my breast you hear them go,*
> *To the relief they bring my life I owe*
> *Since I should die of sorrow otherwise . . .*
> La Vita Nuova
> Dante

I wanted to see if I was still alive, if I could be, ever. Six months after my Gail died I flew to Greece to spend two weeks with close friends, Russ Kordas and Laura Hussey, both accomplished painters, at their splendid, unpretentious rambling white-washed house on the magic ancient island, Samos.

This outcry is a series of postcards, ways of speaking to Gail because I had to, acting as if she were still traveling with me. They surged into life as I tried to tell my lost friend and lover what was happening around me, within me. When Gail was diagnosed, I promised myself I would do two things— everything possible, at any cost and anywhere in the world, to save her life; and if in the end that wasn't possible, then I would help Gail complete her beautiful life in a poetic, gentle, protected, dignified and adventurous way— just as she had lived it. After two years, it turned out the second road was the one.

When I journeyed to Samos the first time, two year's worth of pent-up suffering and 24/7 attention focused on my loving friend, exploded into words, into the world.

It was pathetic, horrible, miserable, pitiful, laughable, some might say unmanly; it was cathartic, volcanic, a bit mad as well as maddening, inescapably serious, yet utter folly.

It just happened.

I was trying to make believe Gail was on the road with me, or I actually thought she was, or maybe I was unable to be without thinking she was still beside me.

I was compelled to recount each moment and sensation of my trip to the Mediterranean, and in telling my lost love so many mundane and miraculous stories, I see I was ferociously and unconsciously fighting the inevitable forgetting that comes upon us all, no matter how strong or acute our memories and spirits.

I was summing up a story I did not want to end.

I did not want to let her go, so I just told her stories. It was that simple, I guess.

But that's how love goes, especially lost love, love ripped from your heart, blown-up love, detonated love, love burnt to a crisp by the fires of life, a life miraculous and indifferent, charmed and cursed, blessed and nothing more than a cosmic joke.

These poems meander, are elliptical, interrelated, go nowhere and somewhere at the same time, they are loose-fitting, circular, baggy, skittish, edgy, un-tethered. Well, my mind was so unsteady, traveled back and forth in time and place, within a day, within hours of the same day, from dreams to the overcharged living reality before me, over a lifetime, centuries. Half the time, I didn't know where I was although to the world I seemed perfectly fine, simply a tourist from America, like others, except that this guy never took off his Ray Bans or the baseball cap tucked tight over his forehead.

I desperately tried to hang on, to passages in books, to lyrics of familiar songs, to melodies I knew. Songs by Stevie Wonder, James Taylor, Bach, Gram Parsons, Elton John, Neil Young, Dvorak, Mahler, Brahms, Paul Simon, Mozart, Robert Johnson, Dylan, Ella, Jobim, Little Walter, Judy Collins, Joan Baez, Jimmy Webb, Muddy Waters, gypsy songs, Billy Eckstine, Etta James,

Jackson Browne, Selena, so many others; they were my melodic prosthetics enabling my mind and soul to walk a bit further.

I leaned upon the dazzling Mediterranean world sparkling and waving around me, and especially, I clutched so many vibrant memories, which cast themselves unannounced, wave after wave, upon the shore of my mind, because they needed to be experienced again, to be consumed, digested, internalized within each cell of my being. I needed to see my love again, and the adventure-filled road we had taken, if only to throw it into the ocean like a small bottle with a deep and special message within, written by a child, so serious and so lost, scrawled in tides of emotion and with indelible script.

I didn't know any other way on the first trip to Samos— you see, we were *always* talking. Gail and I, her voice and thoughts, her insights, had become part of me, we lived in a syncopated way, two counterpointed, similar/different people who had found each other somehow by chance, sharing, being together, for decades, around the world. Neither of us had regrets about anything— nothing was left unfinished, except perhaps one more stroll around Rome.

Just living each day, we are all on a great battle field called life, whether we know it or not. And when someone you love dies, you have to die yourself, countless times, you really must face up to the miserable cold fact of death which is really life itself come calling but in a tragic way, the splitting apart of you from the person you love perhaps more than your own life, and you just have to give it up, this life, the life you had together, what only you two knew and loved. And you have to give it up it many times, surrender the magic world of your empire of love countless bloody times in order to be reborn. And if you are brave enough, and stubborn and lucky enough, you will survive, you will be reborn, you will find freedom and sunrise, new ways of being and living and falling in love.

All lovers in the end are parted though true love does endure. Your heart is ripped from your chest. And you run after it, hold it quivering in your wet, scarlet hands, and you plant your still beating heart into the forgiving earth, and it grows like an immense, singular tree with songs of love and promise that you could never have imagined.

Only the most devastating pain brings marvels into this world. Only utter sorrow carries with it flowers of such powerful fragrance. Who knew? Who could tell us really?

But at first there is nothing, nothing at all in the entire universe, only intense, aching suffering and loss—utter ruin and confusion. It's all about the pain, and how you handle it, curiously turn it over and over like a stone you find in the park, in the woods, or as you will read, like the white stone I found in the sea, until pain itself begins to slowly disappear, become something unexpected in your scarred lover's hands of golden magic and tears.

After crying out for so long like a newborn baby, you do finally stop, you catch your breath, and startled, you look at the new world around. This comes much later; after storms of grief, after you act like a fool so many times, act unfairly to friends and lovers, totally out of control, rude and cold. You are lost and trying to hang on.

But it comes to you, this new life, if you want it badly enough, act crazy enough, if you pray with enough faith, diligence and desperation, and finger the wounds and scars with enough care and compassion and attention.

Listen, it does come back again. Life comes back again. And love does, too.

You do become yourself again.

But, you don't really, become yourself again. You are changed forever; your heart and soul and spirit are transformed into a kind of razor sharp love blade that cuts through life in an undeniable yet compassionate way.

You become someone very different, maybe better, perhaps even greater.

Because of all the pain, because of what has happened to you, and what happened to her, this person you loved and prized above all others, because of how love goes.

The airport waiting room is empty except for me.
Jerry Jeff Walker sings a live version of *One Too Many Mornings*.
(I remember you said he was from Upstate and that you heard him
in Jefferson at the Heartbreak by the green.)
The excited audience, the sound of clapping, perfect for Dylan's sorrowful classic
which I associate with wandering the streets of the West Village,
open-hearted and joyous, transfigured in glistening early mornings,
around the time you had that apartment with Debbie on West 13th Street.
But glued to this plastic row chair, bucket seat into the unknown,
I realize that in all those countless songs we loved
this is what they meant by *broken hearts*.
The Mediterranean sun outside burns eternal midday
into dark mountains at the far edge of the bleached black cracking cement tarmac.
A couple of families sat around me for a while.
A slim pale girl her straight black hair pulled back
stepped right out of a Pompeian fresco.
Bent old couples nested in chairs, their gnarled hands touched.
A short dark guy grooved to his iPod.
They are all gone now, they left on the last flight.
We fight to use whatever influence we can muster
to get the best seats for a meal, a show, a flight, a film,
to get ahead on line after line snaking through the customs of life.
But in the end, let's face it, the seats aren't really ours baby,
and we have to give them up so strangers can take our places.
There's nobody here to buy a Coke or sandwich at the small Autogrill.
Cocky young guys in blue airport vests
strut and wave their phallic security wands.
But they don't bother to double check me.
I look too harmless or lost or absent I guess.
In all the places we traveled darling—
Paris, Madrid, in Barcelona, in Rome,
they're all eating Sunday dinners, clattering dishes,
drinking wine, arguing politics, laughing at hilarious stories.
I can hear them all from where I sit beneath the whooshing A/C
on this side of *the lonesome ocean*.
I listen to one of our favorite songs,
remember those last days together.

When I Was in New York

That afternoon you sat on the couch
Spanish Boots of Spanish Leather played on the boom box,
and you gazed into my eyes and said so gravely,
Gar, it's a song of parting,
then stared at the ceiling,
not wanting to cry in front of our smiling marvelous Emily.
By myself with you so far away sweetheart
I pray we do stay *forever young* like that other song says.
But right at this moment with earphones in my head and nobody around,
it takes all I've got to stay upright and headed into bliss.

Misty gray shadow mountains
and I lovingly call your name in the sun.
Cicadas sing softly in their home in paradise.
The tops of two cypresses dance for us my love,
waving and weaving like good luck ravens above my head.
Without you the wine tastes so different and I sigh so often,
on my walks, on mad taxi rides around hair-pin turns,
up and down mountain roads lined with memorials
to drivers who miraculously made it.
Paradise is still here I am happy to report,
but it is infinitely poorer and so much sadder
without your beaming smile, your soft siesta embraces,
the way you pored over maps and through tour books
recounting bits of history spiced with your telling insights,
part of our continual, comical unspoken self-improvement program.
On a walk with Russ this morning overlooking the Aegean
we stopped beside a grotto where a huge eucalyptus stood before its final storm.
And Russ said it was unjust that you had to go so soon
because you were so connected to flowers, to books, to food and wine
because you were in the middle of your life's journey
with your hungry intensity and gentle compassion.
When I got up this morning I felt you next to me
under the walnut tree, beneath the almond, the pear, the olive, the wild fig.
My skin bakes, my heart aches, flies buzz in the dry grass.
This trip to paradise pain has sidled up smiling
intent upon being my constant companion.

Russ and Laura's white-washed Samos home overlooks the Aegean, sits within
ancient stone-walled, terraced gardens with fruit trees, grapevines, morning
glories, two abandoned wells. A small pale blue bedroom was my nighttime
refuge. Populating the house: piles and shelves of yellowing paperbacks and
dusty hard covers, four wooden chairs around the kitchen table, Russ and
Laura's drawings and paintings, classical music CDs stacked like leaning piles
of dessert dishes. Two grand cypresses stand to the left as you sit facing the
sea. I watched these magnificent trees day and night from the small white
balcony outside my blue room and from the gardens.

The towering cypresses sway in afternoon heat.
Swallows soar on sea breezes.
Waves faintly crash against the far away shore.
I think that's an owl hooting
in time to the rhythm of the cicadas.
Close my eyes,
open them again,
sweat in the sun,
murmur,
Thank you.
Thank you.

Men and women
leave wakes
that persist
for a time
but finally
disappear.

Sweetheart it's nighttime on Samos.
A voice whistles to a barking dog.
The neighbor across the olive grove mops the porch.
Invisible cars rumble by.
Unseen cicadas keep me company from sunrise
till it's too late to stay awake anymore.
Sea winds cool my chest and scalp.
If I wonder why I made it back
this is the answer,
what's around me
at this moment
as I write
these words to you.

I never thought I would return
to the old stone walls by the plum tree
next to the wild fig and the walnut grown so huge
since that year giggling like kids
we piled seven of the heaviest rocks
we could find onto the green cover of the well.
The green paint bubbles,
the thick branches are bleached
from relentless sun and wild winter storms.
Brambles grow along
rusted metal edges.
Dry grass and thorns blanket the wooden cover.
Standing in grass littered with rotting pears
I can see our life then
how we laughed, drank wine, ate olives and fresh bread
with friends and family on the terrace garden,
the world so light, electric and open-ended,
before we had to close up the house
that final season.
How could I know that I would come back
years later alone,
stand like a statue planted in sacred ground
beside the old green well
we closed for good
because it just ran out of water one day.

The two dark cypresses
know for certain,
dance in the morning bay breeze,
at night wave unseen
as I try to fall asleep
in the pale blue room
praying to dream of you.

If you didn't know the sun
who would ever believe
that luminous dying orange splotch
far out on the dark purple horizon
is actually the source of all life.

I cried again in the pale blue room
in the dark as the dog barked outside
and drunken kids shouted.
I wish I could dance with you again my love
in that funky country road house Upstate.
I wish we could make love in the pasture above the valley
on a bed of wild oregano in the early summer sun on a walk,
just the two of us joyous in a lost jukebox world of country ballads and rock and roll,
with cold bottles of beer sweating and boot heels flashing.
I sense you're still with me
as I stagger and plunge through the aftermath of losing you.
Balanced in the icy clear water this morning
on my back, belly to the sun, ears under water,
I whispered,
I love you.
I love you.

I craved music on my first journey to Samos. I needed a soundtrack, familiar and painful and filled with memories that stabbed me like melodic daggers hour by hour. I needed my music fix to try to settle and inspire me, to guide me, a blind man crawling through life after the detonation of his world, after the destruction of the city of his soul and mind. I was hooked to music as I made my first forays into a distant, uncharted land that was, I gradually came to understand, my new norm, my new homeland. Life without her, life without, just that, without, life without. So I leaned on Sinatra, and the Stones and U2 and Horowitz, Sam Cooke, Coleman Hawkins, Victor Jara, Linda Ronstadt and Emmylou Harris, Curtis Mayfield, Harry Nilsson, Glenn Gould, Paul Simon, Aznavour and BB King. Tony Bennett and Elmore James held me upright.

The sun is shining although it's raining in my heart.
The sun is shining although it's raining in my heart.
I'm in love with my baby
And I hate to see us part.
Dreams end the way the orange sun descends
from the cement terrace over the darkening bay
like a forlorn golden dove into the sea each day.

The Albanian workmen will come again tomorrow
to repair the façade of the white-washed house,
brush fine marble mixed with cement on the cracked walls.
When they finish we'll sweep and hose down the floors.
Then we can fill our glasses with wine,
watch the close of patient, mysterious days
spent together in this enchanted garden
painted by stubborn strong hands
at the top of a luminous world
protected from the ravages of time
and the unsettled hearts of men.

Nearly every day I took crazy local cabs to Mykali Beach, which I had
discovered with Gail several years before when we stopped to see Russ and
Laura with our kids, Danny and Emily. Russ wasn't well at the time, and
our two friends remained in Athens and didn't make their annual summer
pilgrimage to Samos. So the three of us wandered around the island, and I
took a steady flow of real time phone directions from Russ back in Piraeus
about what we should see and do, as if he and Laura were with us. Mykali was
still astounding; the place of the transfiguration of all bathers, whether they
knew it or not.

At daybreak I bathe in joyous electric light.
The dark bay shivers whitecaps.
I smile, remember
how you taught me
to love the morning.
How could that glistening blonde couple
know
standing chest-high in the sea,
gloriously beautiful
that they are actually posing
this unnoticed ordinary instant,
holding hands
for an eternity snapshot.

The sea streams through heavy curtains
to kiss me as I cry in the small blue room.
Even with earphones and Clapton wailing *Reconsider Baby*
I hear the insistent low voice of the waves
rolling onto the rocks on the beach.
I'd like to write you a letter my love
about how much I miss you, how much fun we would have
again at blessed Mykali Beach,
about the erudite Greek taxi driver who lived
in Australia, about the wild cats who gingerly step into the kitchen
now that the big white house is open for summer,
about the chill of the Aegean,
how the water clasps the nape of my neck,
the whoosh-whoosh of my breathing as I float
on my back, the wine in the restaurants, the cold beer,
the swallows rocketing at dusk, the dog barking
as I write weeping with the small reading lamp on,
Bach and Renee Fleming playing downstairs.
About how we ate a simple spaghetti dinner a while ago,
talked politics, about the fate of our poor planet,
about whether the Albanian workers did a good job fixing the walls,
and how much more is left to be done.
Yes I'd like to write so much to you sweetheart,
about how you can still careen up tan hills in cabs
and suddenly the sea leaps right at you,
about the derelict ancient walls on the sides of dry winding roads,
the terraces of olive groves abandoned
to fend for themselves for centuries,
how from these magic hills scented with jasmine,
the families of vintners and shepherds fled long ago.
How from time to time you glimpse shed-sized empty white chapels
with no one left to pray
for good crops, for safe passage on the fickle sea.
And there's so much to say about these two tall cypresses
that guard me day and night outside the house,
the wide regal walnut framed in the bathroom window,
the mysterious abandoned well,

how I shook the pear tree and was bombarded with fruit,
the cloud of tan butterflies bouncing in the dry brown grass,
the morning glories that dare to awaken each day,
the smell of eucalyptus, the steep narrow cement street
we scale to leave and return to the house.
The Dutch, Greek and English families at the beach laugh.
Old couples carefully hold hands in the surf.
So much to tell you dear, to explain about this trip
back to paradise, this bitter exhilarating time.
I'd have to write so many volumes baby
to capture a tenth of what we spoke about all the time.
Yes I would have to write so many pages
and something else, dear—I need your new address
so you can receive each postcard I write
because I know you would want them,
that if you were here beside me, you'd be writing them too.
PS: Flying in over ancient Samos
I'm probably the first visitor to this land
of Pythagoras and the great Temple of Hera
who listened to Elmore James sing *Crossroads*.
Thought you'd get a kick out of that.

I stood in the small bathroom shed at the beach, singing to myself, looking out
a narrow horizontal window.

Behind the fir trees the palms wave.
A sad love song I can't understand plays.
The sun burns through mist.
Mountains emerge purple, regal, observant.
Swimming in cold currents
of the straits between two worlds
I 'm electrified by all that I know and feel
no more or less, than this—
Paradise is here,
right here and now,
where you are
I am—right now.
The cicadas serenade me in the heat.

There are only times and places and people,
dreams abandoned or rescued from the ruins of forgetfulness
like exotic piazzas stumbled upon in the noonday sun,
empty, stark, brilliantly lit and pregnant with meaning,
at the precise instant when you find yourself
traveling alone or with a friend at the X-marks-the-spot,
when you are so far from home that no one you ever knew
has any idea exactly where you are and your heart beats
in time to this fantastic responsibility— the undying hunger
to see, to live feeling compelled to experience life
with delirious and sacred fires raging
and to be able to send streams of shimmering blue postcards
jotted down hastily back to friends, family, and lovers
from a priceless journey that is really the molten core
of life itself on this planet earth
this life vacation, this excursion into our world.

At the beach, when I wasn't reading, sleeping or drowning into myself, I watched tourists, families, couples, kids, all from an immense distance. I felt as if I had landed on earth from outer space. I was the man on the moon come to see what humans do with the carefree moments of their fleeting lives.

I was no longer part of this world. I was separated, cut off from men and women, from the give and take, the push and pull of living. I *regarded* men and women; I *observed* their habits, their behavior. It had nothing, and everything, to do with me.

Every single person or thing I saw or smelled or heard, I felt within the burnt, savaged core of what was left of me. Every single thing and moment was pregnant with immense meaning and importance; each image, scent, and feeling exploded into millions of vivid and dramatic movies spinning back and forth in time, reels of heartache, spools of ecstasy, endless fields planted with my tattered bloody flags lost love.

I was trying to understand the daily language of a reason to continue being in the world, attempting to decode the significance to everything I was experiencing, to discover like an explorer in a strange new world what life meant, or might mean, to someone like me, solo flying, wandering to and fro in search of the sacred fire within, to come upon it somewhere somehow, and to gently fan the embers if I could, in the hope that one day, far in the future, unseen but fully imagined on this terrible and glorious trip to paradise, one day my inner fire would roar again.

I was shaken by every incandescent object and gesture on Samos. I was uplifted and reminded of my insignificance by the eternal sea, the sun, the overarching sky. How many broken, desperate lovers had come to the sea? What is love really in the face of the sea, under the all-seeing sun?

They seem so slight, so vulnerable and young
walking gingerly on the slick stones into the sea.
Before they enter the cold clean water
I see that he rubs her white taught belly
reassuringly with his left hand.
They're embracing now.
The wise Aegean rises to her nipples.
His huge Buddy Holly shades reflect the sun.
The distant mountains laugh as they kiss.
Cicadas sing fleeting love songs that
dart like meadow larks through the rustling bamboo.
They don't hear, but how could they?

I took a ferry to Kousadasi, a port in Turkey to visit the nearby ancient ruins at Ephesus. The trip turned into a misadventure since I missed the tour bus once we landed in Turkey. (Four years later when I returned to Samos, I had no problem finding the bus which was parked literally outside the door of the ferry station in Kusadasi, the port where you dock in Turkey.) I was obviously lost, confused. But because I missed the bus, I was free to wander Kusadasi, which flowered for me, taught me.

The leafy late morning park here is much livelier
than baking ruins thousands of years old.
The Turkish family at the next table
eats the same breakfast I wolf down.
How could that macho thieving Turkish tour guide
realize that by arguing with me about
how I wasn't smart enough to catch the tour bus

to Ephesus with the rest of the visitors to Kusadasi
that he gave me the greatest gift possible—
time to watch this impatient hungry kid
rock in his chair and clank his silverware,
wonder at that bent old man on the park bench as he sips tea beside his motorbike,
relish the ravishing dim-witted girl in the tourist office,
her brown eyes huge and empty enough to hold worlds.
The floppy heart-shaped leaves above my head
send soft circles of yellow-gold sunlight
to dance on the carmine table cloth by my hands.
Day trips don't always turn out as we planned.
Life trips also defy our will,
unpredictable like the sparkling water that
flies and bounces on the stones in the fountain.
When you feel most lost and angry
somewhere on this earth
rainbows shimmer and bridge worlds
from one frail human heart to another
the distance it takes to draw a breath,
to succumb
to marvels
of simply being alive.

Traveling
alone
without
you
I strain
to be
even more
focused.
Yet I am
lost
so much
more often.

I have had my fill of death,
of magnificent ruins of cities and nations,
dreams imprisoned in stifling hospital waiting rooms.
Cities of the dead have no more to teach me.
I stare at the urgent deep blue sea rush past the rocking ferry.

You flash into my mind, things you said last summer
when we were together at the beach back home.
First, quietly out of nowhere in the restaurant one morning
when there was still hope that you'd make it.
I think that people like me may have to go early
so that people wake up more to life.
The gulls cried overhead and the sun was strong.
I was thunderstruck by your sudden, certain words
since I was living then only to save you.
Another morning at breakfast at our favorite outdoor café,
you said softly in a dreamy voice smiling your eyes half-closed,
Gary, if I made a film it would start that way,
with the gulls and the sound of the sea.
Then later as hope gradually vanished,
walking to lunch during our last trip to Cape May,
as we stepped into the restaurant by the beach
I began to speak in an exaggerated upbeat way
because I saw that you were crying
as you recounted a story you'd read
about the unintended good consequences
that rippled out across the world
because of a woman's simple, compassionate act.
And when you returned from your daily dawn meditation by the Atlantic
I had just gotten up and brushed my hair.
Your eyes glowed, my love, your skin radiant
from the vision that you had been granted.
The sunrise made everything purple, Gar—
Everything, and then I saw the dolphins leaping
with such joy, and standing in the water I was able
to remember all the other times I had been in the sea,
in Sardinia, in Corsica, Mykali Beach, Miami, here in Cape May.
I was able in that instant to be in all these places again.
After you spoke I held your peony face,
kissed you gently, held on to you.
As I write the cold spray wets my face
in the late day Aegean sun and wind.
I cry beneath my sunglasses on the ferry,

struggling for air on the wide white wooden bench.
Our stubborn passionate tears
flavor the wine dark sea
with its bracing, reassuring magic
so one day it tickles us out of nowhere
and we can laugh again.

In my pale blue bedroom, or sitting at Mykali Beach, on walks, in the garden,
lying awake nights in bed, I'd play the music I brought with me— and I was
off, out there, flying into the past, trying to comprehend and digest what had
happened. I wrestled with my own special angel the entire journey to Samos.
We fought, my angel and I, how we tried to overcome each other night and
day, and we grappled with Miles Davis, Roy Orbison, Brel, Johnny Cash, Bill
Evans and Duke Ellington serenading our warring, restless, wayward hearts,
our determined, killer minds.

My thoughts raced back and forth through time. I circled over and over scenes
from my life with Gail, which to my disbelief, were lost forever in the physical
world. Despite my will, I was forced to sum up what our life together had meant,
to sketch the lines and colors of all the picture postcard perfect moments that
I had shared with her. I had no idea where I was really, or where I was headed,
whether any of it mattered at all.

Evening comes,
I play a splendid song
of parting by Dylan.
The neighbor's dog barks in the night.
I see the crescent moon rise over the bay
through the coarse white curtains of the small blue room.
I'm still unable to read anything of substance
which I know must be hard for you to believe
because I always suffered like you from "book hunger."
I'm beginning to nod out on the narrow, hard bed as I write.
I'm not sure if I'm listening to Chet Baker, the Beatles,
Sinatra, Muddy Waters or Stan Getz,
if my tears have splashed off my legs and the sheets,

right out the windows, flown like swallows over the white-washed balcony
across the sea to the far black mountains
which the locals believe resemble a long ago great king and queen
now lying in profile and waiting to awaken one day.
I'm not sure how long I've been sleeping.
Cross-legged I check the time on my red travel clock.
I slowly stand, brush my teeth, wash my face,
hide back under the covers and think of what used to happen now:
Good night, my love,
I said countless times to you
around the world before we fell asleep.
Good night, baby,
you always answered,
your radiant face inches from mine.
Then this, always, softly from you:
Rest now dear . . . Rest.
And I would then,
I could then.
Breathing heavily, my tears won't stop.
Far away the waves wash in and out.
And there's that dog barking again.

My great love I imagine these postcards I send
from the edges of my journeying life
may one day slow, perhaps stop altogether.
But I know I will always be writing to you
with the stubborn gentleness of my beating heart,
with the tireless in and out of my breath,
with the quiet persistence of the morning glories
which flourish on this enchanted island,
with words deep blue and blissful,
always mindful,
joyously opening each sunrise
silently closing as dusk comes on,
relentless, grateful and faithful,
growing wild and bold on rocks facing the sea.

Postcard memory from long ago
that I never told you dear—
When you had gone to the restroom in the café in Rome.
Her body will change, said the stocky, bald man in his 60s,
done up in dark sunglasses and a rakish open short sleeve shirt.
Transfixed by his sudden attention I wondered if he was a famous director or artist.
She is beautiful— inside and outside, he said with his heavy Italian accent,
staring right into me, so deeply I still feel that gaze.
Her body will change but always remember her beauty.
Then you returned beaming because we were traveling together on the Open Road.
And the stranger vanished, buried again in the morning paper.
When you are in your 20s and in love,
exploding with visions, dreams, ideas,
streams of romantic, urgent words, images, hopes,
I guess it's possible, even forgivable, to forget or discount,
what a solitary "old man" in the corner of a neighborhood cafe sternly advises.
But I never did forget
and decades later alone and in anguish,
balanced with you on the edge of life and death,
I saw his worldly Roman face again lit as a movie on the hospital wall,
sitting beside your bed that night as our world fell apart.
The old man miraculously returned
as you slept and we were there again in our favorite café by the train station,
a few blocks from the incandescent Pension Pezzotti.
And even with all the horror and pain,
the day by day dismantling of our cherished and glittering world,
the unexpected storm uprooting our world of love,
the shattering of my heart, medical test after painful medical test,
bad news after bad news, in waiting rooms, days and nights without air,
reading poetry and holding your hand in hospital rooms,
in bed at night exhausted, crying alone under the covers,
so you and the kids couldn't hear,
I summoned the undying buoyancy of that joyous Italian time
like the chocolate froth on a cup of cappuccino
in that modest neighborhood café where
round ruddy Botero waiters glowed with pride
as they brought each fabulous, simple dish,

where we held hands, kissed and whispered
about our plans for the coming day's adventures,
how we launched ourselves into paintings and buildings,
where smiling nuns with huge white wings
ate heaping plates of fish and fresh fruit on ice,
where North African peddlers wolfed down pasta and wine,
and where tough local bookies wagered
each day on who would win in the end.

To whom can I offer all these words my lost love,
what I see on the horizon of my mind.
Your blue eyes gray like the serious sea,
your sensual mouth so modest and devout,
your inexpensive black cotton dress in the Roman sun,
the way you crossed your legs in Parisian cafes,
how you radiated joy in your yellow
summer dress with little purple flowers,
how we made love in simple pensions and small hotels,
ate salami and drank wine in our rooms,
read in bed, on trains, in planes, in cafes, in fields.
Who can I tell about the cans of sardines
we had that night by the Seine when we were broke,
how we rationed ourselves to one small sandwich each day,
those tunas on small rolls with hot sauce called Tunisian Delights,
and just one croissant and one café each in the morning,
and yet we still explored Paris on foot from dawn till night.
How we bumped into an elderly French cleaning lady,
the brilliant Madame Papazian, in her rough blue smock,
self-taught, querulous, sharp like a small hawk,
married to an equally amazing Armenian gentleman she called *Papaz*.
How Madame immediately took us under her wing,
grilled me like a cultural machine gun about literature and history and philosophy,
on the overnight train to Spain from Paris while you sensibly slept.
And finally satisfied as we passed the Crusader castle at Carcasson,
Madame shouted suddenly in French to a young local guys loitering between cars,
This is an Occidental Man!
This young American is an Occidental Man!

And later how Madame gave us a tour of Paris
These are prostitutes, my young Americans!
she shouted in French in Pigalle pointing at the smiling girls.
These are prostitutes!
How we spied Sartre and Ionesco in cafes when we had no money.
How we stood on rickety chairs in that damp seedy Left Bank hotel
and declaimed *Song of Myself* to a befuddled Czech couple.
To whom can I show the tender way you'd pet me back
to sleep after a nightmare,
or that never-to-be-forgotten Thanksgiving we spent in Milan,
how we hitchhiked in a blizzard back to Rome
in the rattling fish truck with the smiling driver from the Abruzzi
who looked exactly like the beatific father in *Bicycle Thief.*
How he let us climb into his cab
and said sweetly in Italian shaking his head,
Only two Americans would hitchhike in a blizzard.
How he handed us bubble gum, Ella Fitzgerald and Liza Mainelli on the radio,
how I spoke French and broken Italian with him and explained
how everybody we knew back home was eating turkey.
(Last year you said this was one of your most treasured memories.)
Who else but you can truly *understand*
what the apparent laziness of this café I'm sitting in right now *really* signifies,
so similar to the deceptive, easygoing nature of the fabulous blue sea.
Who will ever really comprehend your quiet morning excitement
on our endless walks around strange cities,
how your eyes always lit and grew larger with childlike wonder
when our plane took off on another journey.
Who will ever visit our lost glittering empire of love,
ringing with laughter, conversation, sighs and dreaming.
I guess that's why I write these postcards
from the Taverna Scopos at Mykali Beach,
why I come each day and drink until I can't anymore,
hide with my shades on, draw on white paper placemats,
vibrate with cicadas, watch the tourists lounge,
bathe in sorrowful Greek love songs on the sound system.
I guess that's why my love. I guess that's why.

Poems,
chiseled pain
carved
into my restless
lonely heart.

Forcing myself to return to paradise
I remember the ancient maxim—
Know thyself
inscribed on the floor of the oracle at Delphi,
and also written by hand by you on a small piece of lined paper
over two decades ago for me to keep
in my top desk drawer at work
a reminder of the importance of living well.
Sigh by sigh, smile by smile, breath by breath,
we get closer to our true nature,
and so the world awakens with joy.
How I miss you darling.

At first
I thought I saw
three zones in the sea
leading to the infinite
horizon.
But the longer
I looked
the more I saw
the grays in the greens
that there are no
blacks and whites
in the blues.

I learned the other day that blessed Mykali Beach under me now
was laid with landmines not too many years ago
to destroy Turkish invaders from across the straits.
But after a while no one showed so the locals removed the explosives
and men and women rediscovered the magic of the sea.

After a while without fanfare a few shacks sprouted for a trickle of tourists,
and so here I am once again in paradise by the Aegean.
A creamy cover of clouds and mist flowed over Samos this morning.
But now it's burned into non-existence
by the unforgiving, all-knowing sun.
Most of the lounge chairs are empty today baby.
The hazy sun fades away to my right.
You never get over something like that.
You just go on living, our wild friend Russ
explained on the phone to a crony who inquired about my current visit.
I guess this is what it's all about sweetheart,
remembering and yet finding strength
enough to forget
so that the countless smooth stones of our love
that for no reason vomited into the universe like a cataclysmic life volcano
are able to connect magically above me
a glittering protective umbrella of see-through sorrow
rather than bury me
under layers of impenetrable suffocating dead rock.

On the way to the beach, Russ and Laura took me to small villages, where we
had lunch; classic, fairy tale Vourliotes, nests on a mountainside of cool pines
and cypresses, sheltered from the sun.

You cannot tell the sky from the sea
when you reach such heights.
The village called Vourliotes rests
on mountains, olive groves,
terraces of deep green cypress.
We had lunch in the Blue Chairs restaurant
in a square with overhanging grape vines.
A two-year-old boy named Alexander,
related to the owners,
climbed up and down the restaurant's steep steps.
The white beans in tomato sauce were excellent.
The spinach croquets over done, the dolmades dry.
During lunch, which you would have loved,

Laura explained that as a couple
friends apparently always described us this way:
Everybody likes Gary and Gail.
Shifting in my seat, I realize that
from now on it's just: *Gary* . . .
me alone— just me from now on.
Where are you when I need you, sweetheart?
Once I think I get over the hump of parting,
I'm floored again, strangled, crushed,
by the sudden comprehension
you are not here with me
in paradise, walking around New York,
Upstate in the woods, watching the stars,
sitting beside me in cafes, by the sea,
that you are gone forever,
that you will never again play around
with life, with me,
that you are somewhere
out there
on the wide sea
but unlike Odysseus you will never make it home again.
I mean this earthbound home where I still live.
Our two friends are taking such fine care of me,
cook fantastic meals, food shop, buy wine I like.
Laura's even going to bake me one of her famous apple pies.
Russ is planning to cook a huge fish we bought at the market this morning.
But there is so much I have to do to prepare
for a life without you.
After more beer and wine our gentle huge driver
who resembles Luca Brazzi in *The Godfather,*
said that today between pick-ups
he stopped the car three times to swim.
Luca drove me to Mykali Beach with Greek music playing
in his cozy air conditioned Toyota sedan.
As I write to you I whimper like a child.
Even under an umbrella the relentless sun penetrates deep
into the darkest parts
of what is left of me.

I usually stayed at Mykali at the Scopos Taverna till everyone had gone. Alone, the breeze getting chilly in the late afternoon, coming out of my own interior world, it would finally dawn on me that I was alone and the beach was deserted. With a towel around my shoulders, I'd ask at the taverna for a taxi back to the house.

I never took off my sunglasses on the first trip to Samos, even in the sea. Though I wanted to be in paradise, and I needed to be among people, to be reminded about what life was all about, I desperately had to hide myself like a wounded animal in a dark, protected cave, shield my eyes from the gaze of others. For I was blind, shocked into darkness, because my eyes had witnessed the flash of the atomic bombing of the world of my love, the center of my heart, the core of my soul. And I knew, as I wrestled with my dark angel, that I had to get that shocked ground zero look out of my eyes. I had to awaken my frozen face, and loosen my stony, unmoving, cartoon smile. I knew that one day I would have to laugh again, joyously, with gratitude, let go, let it go. But for now, I was within the furnace of my own stormy grief, right in the center of the chaotic and serene whirlwind.

There's nobody here anymore
at Mykali beach at sunset.
Blinded by light
I see so clearly we grew up together,
learned to mouth passionate vowels
of living side by side wandering the world,
stubborn consonants of ideas that won't seem to die.
We conjugated life in every tense baby,
wherever we were, wherever we could get to next,
laughing, loving, musing, toasting, dreaming
with the microscopic specificity and universal vision
of what it takes to be fully alive.
As I walk I follow my elongated shadow along the shore.
Millions of stones like stars
hint there are worlds and worlds washed beyond the foam.
The smiling mountains across the water have witnessed
nations cry and laugh and rage and disappear.
A Native American jeweler I met back home

was advised by his Elders
after he lost his teenage daughter in a car crash
that he had to let her spirit go
so that after one year's time his dear girl's soul
could find its way to the Land of Great Spirits.
The waves at my feet tell me to follow this way.
Water scallops roll melodically with bubbles and spray.
This day's light vanishes slowly.
The sea wind grows.
It's time to return home to our friends.
One day I will release you,
fly away for good, dear.
Yet I know you'll remain forever
with me in love,
as I continue to trail
my crooked early evening shadow
on the rocks washed by the sea.

When people die, we can still speak to them. Why not? So, I talked to Gail all
the time since it was my way of being in the world; we had talked and loved for
decades without let up. When someone who matters does what we call "die,"
a special way of talking to life ends, a way of dancing with life packs up and
moves away. If you are lucky all you possessed becomes an inner dialogue,
unnoticed most times, becomes part of your very being and it continues as
long as you continue to breathe, for as long as your heart beats. Lovers are all
separated in the end but their love talk goes on forever.

Honey for some reason here at Mykali
I again had to relive that day we sat by the Seine hungry
so young, eating canned sardines.
Ever organized we rationed one croissant and just one cafe
for each of us daily yet we still marched all over Paris,
and then through Barcelona and Madrid
and finally the fabulous city we both thought we had inhabited
in another life long ago— wayward, intricate, undulating, undying Rome.
On the road we encountered angels, heroes, geniuses and fools,
saw miracles and experienced mornings fresh

enchanted like all those the fairy tales you knew by heart.
We held hands and wondered our way
along meandering electric highways ravenous
with flowering kisses, towering citadels and sculptures,
starry fields of incense, rivers flowing lazily
to exotic seas swirling purple through tough sexy film noir port cities,
neon songs ringing blue in so many seedy, romantic downtowns,
the musky sacred precincts we shared noontimes in cool shade.
Homesickness some Sunday afternoons no family dinners to enjoy,
racing to catch trains to new countries,
carrying cream puffs to elderly nuns,
licking ice cream cones in lush gardens like kids,
scaling cathedrals, hitchhiking in blizzards with fishmongers going south,
making love in countless beds around the world,
napping while you read beside me,
being surprised when we found out that
fresh loaves of bread, butter, jam and coffee
actually came with that first sleazy room I finagled on the Left Bank.
Buying fresh apricots still warm from the sun on the street,
deciding all of a sudden to sit in a café all day and miss our train
so we could entertain each other with literature,
philosophy, the notion that it's important to
find out what life really means in the end.
And in my mind for some reason a few minutes ago in the blinding heat
I saw those huge joyous snowflakes
silently fall to earth again outside the high arched windows
of the San Marco Monastery in Florence
where Fra Angelico painted the holy cells brilliant celestial blues,
when we were detonated youngsters in love
drank a bottle of local red wine and ate breaded chicken cutlets
on Dante's tomb and toasted the Italian bard,
and recited Whitman for him and laughed and planned more adventures
which of course we were convinced would miraculously happen and last forever.
Though now shadows from the large beach chair
beside me at Mykali Beach creep
across my legs, over chest, into my face.
On the sand so near boys and girls too young to understand

that carefree days of freedom at the beach do really end
shout and splash in their eternal world.
Darling I will forever be buying you
those inexpensive paisley purple
fringed scarves on the street on the Left Bank
under a young sun.
And you will always be wearing them in all your magnificent youthful
beauty, smiling, shy and unpretentious, pure,
so alive, for all time,
if only for me, your comerado,
if only for my broken, lost, manly heart.

The half moon rises on my left.
The fiery white sun gradually
lands upon the sea growing dark blue, then black.
Two gray doves shoot into pines
across from the white-washed balcony
where I sit thinking of you.
The olive and pomegranate trees,
the great walnut and the cypresses,
wave in the soft cicada-bathed night.
I know it makes no sense for me to go on
wondering why you couldn't stick around any longer.
Like on that sad night holding your hand,
I am only able to echo your simple reply to me:
Gary, that's the way it is.
But the sound of the sea winds play in the leaves all around me,
the golden hush of this sacred moment after a nap and shower,
the certainty that we would have made love
this afternoon in my small pale blue room.
The undeniable force of your gentle fierce love
lost somewhere out there yet ever present,
convinces me there is so much more
to lovers parting than having to let each other go,
that if I could really open my eyes I'd see
more clearly that the world's always smiling
and that we have to reply calmly, naturally,

beaming right back like waterfalls of morning glories
cascading rainbow-like onto the rocks of life,
not asking why,
never having to.

The ancient King and Queen of the mountains
slumber in silhouette
across the restless blue bay at dusk.
A few late cars drive by unseen.
Cicadas vibrate paradise in time to their song.
Radios and TVs play somewhere.
Dogs bark and growl.
The wind fondles the fruit trees.
The world rushes, shouts, shoves, and slaughters
yet nothing disturbs the Royal Couple's sleep,
resolved, so the islanders here say,
to awaken one day united in perfect lovers' harmony,
their adventurous warrior life returned,
their wild oregano, eucalyptus kingdom joyous again,
restored for all time,
under the rule of love once more.

The half moon hangs goldenish.
The far shore is ringed with lights.
I can see the stars from my balcony.
You wouldn't know the sea was so alive
unless like tonight the moon decided to light
the relentless, restless, rushing waves.
Walking uphill back from town tonight
I climbed a narrow deserted street by the ocean
and it struck me mid-stride,
hit me again like a thunder fist in my chest
My God, I am alone.
I am totally alone without you.
I staggered, coughed, leaned on a low stone wall,
gulped night air, after a moment, persisted in my ascent,
past tavernas, hotels, loud restaurants and villas.

From the balcony, the two cypresses by the house are vanishing silhouettes.
I can't see the pines where the gray doves nest.
The King and Queen mountains across the bay hide.
Blackness blends into blackness for me now.
Standing in my shorts on the balcony listening to Joan Sutherland
I stare up at the constellations and cry
into endless incomprehensible night
Are you there?
Are you there?
Are you there my love?
I need you.
How I miss you.
I miss you, sweetheart.
Into ancient olive groves indistinguishable from night
Are you there?
I need you.
I love you.
I need you.
Sea breezes cool me,
remind me it's time
to return to the small blue room.
The bottoms of my bare feet are coated with powdery white wash.
I dive into bed moaning
Who cares?
Who cares?
Who cares anymore?
Who cares about anything?

When the world's asleep I peak through the rough
cotton curtains to see if the moon has abandoned me,
to verify that the stars have been extinguished,
that the onrushing sea is stopped at its source,
the birds thrown from their nests,
that morning glories are confused and paralyzed blind,
that mountains have been upturned
and cars launched into fiery violet orbits around the planet.
I carefully open the coarse blue curtains

to learn if this cataclysmic storm raging inside me
has broken out into an unsuspecting world.
But the gay moonlight dances on my fingers,
persistent waves kiss the friendly shore
and so resigned I give up, turn in utter disgust,
fall into my narrow hard bed,
praying to descend
to heights of unknowingness
as swiftly as humanly possible.

It's after my morning walk dear.
I'm sitting on my woven straw Van Gogh chair on the balcony.
The undulating sea is a flawless heavy blue.
I'm wearing my sky blue bathing trunks.
because in an hour or so we're taking a taxi to Mykali Beach.
I wonder if I did get the call after all.
Last night
someone phoned me
or I dreamt it
in paradise,
eyes half-closed.
I grabbed for my cell,
spilled water in the little plastic cup
beside my red traveling clock
onto the pile of books,
Homer, Dante, Alan Watts.
I stretched out on my belly,
fumbled with my cell.
Hello?
Hello?
3:34?
Was it 4:30?
No answer, nothing.
Sighing I lowered my head onto the thin pillow.
Was it you who called last night sweetheart?
When I can't sleep, without you, it's Roy Orbison, Schuman, Mozart, Dexter Gordon,

Curtis Mayfield, the Talking Heads, Springsteen, Nina Simone, David Bowie,
Johnny Cash, Patsy Cline, Warren Zevon, Queen, Willie Nelson, Don Henley,
Leonard Cohen, Beethoven, Judy Garland, the Beach Boys, Vivaldi, Judy
Collins, Callas, more wine, more tears.
I feel my grief might be reaching
a point
where tears don't matter
where stars can't see.
But I'm probably not there yet baby,
not by a long shot,
since the stars still shout with each twinkle
the horror racing around inside their frantic hearts.

The Chicken Place in Samos Town is one of Russ and Laura's favorite local
spots. One night we had dinner there instead of cooking and eating around the
kitchen table.

In the Chicken Place
Laura hummed along with a song
on the sound system.
The Greeks voted this their most
popular song in 100 years.
It's called *Cloudy Sunday* dear.
The songwriter suffered through a long illness Laura explained
so maybe that's why the song's sky darkened.
It's intriguing that a people
who live in pure magical light
chose to honor a song about clouds.
Tonight we walked home from dinner
through dark jasmine-scented streets.
I saw the sensual laughing half-moon
suspended above Samos Town,
the open market where I bought
huge soft peaches for us years ago
near the spartan pension
we stayed to the outrage of the kids
who were used to better digs.

(They ultimately rebelled and
exasperated at my wit's end I said to you
Okay then, let's leave them here.
Let's go to the beach, baby.
And so the two of us discovered sacred
Mykali Beach from where I write to you.)
No doubt you would love
Russ and Laura's rambling white house.
The kids would have played with
the two wild mother cats and their kittens,
explored the gardens and learned how to mix white wash,
how to tell a wild fig from a walnut.
And we all would have bathed in seas that never change.
This house resonates with simple feasts,
feta cheese, fresh loaves of bread, green-golden olive oil,
wine, pyrotechnic conversation and laughter,
arguments and tirades about politics and art,
even Hendrix, Joni Mitchell, Marvin Gaye, the Doors, Smokey Robinson.
(Russ has long decreed a solely Bach household
so I appreciated his special musical dispensation—a kind of knighthood!)
You would get a kick out of hearing
Stevie Wonder blasted over the sleeping roosters,
the vineyards, grape vines, the tacky hotels and soaring cypresses,
way out across the dark valley,
way down into the night
to where you can't see anymore
to the accepting unseen sea.
At night with the floor-to-ceiling kitchen windows thrown open
the doves in the pines near the shore coo in time to *I Was Made to Love Her*,
songs that rock like the never-ending mysterious sea itself,
into black endless fields of winking stars.
As I write this celestial postcard to you
I know that you get what I mean baby.
I swell with fire like the orange hibiscus
I saw today in the noon hour light.
The afternoon sun fingers and searches
Mykali Beach's carpets of smooth significant stones.
Each thing you do in paradise matters for itself alone.

There are day truths
and night truths too,
swelling colorless,
cold and shocking,
within the warm embrace
of the ocean's loving
unfathomable heartbeat.

Losing you
rises unexpectedly
from my true nature.
Explosions,
high-pitched,
almost inaudible,
breathtaking,
choked,
suffocating,
shrieks,
muffled whimpers,
the essence
of what it means,
or used to mean
to be me.

Another night we ate at a pizza restaurant in Samos Town by the port. When
I returned to my small blue room, I brought a sprig of jasmine I plucked for
Gail, in remembrance of her, for me, really for both of us.

Bach's *Partitas* by Glenn Gould downstairs.
Dogs bark, the silent half-full moon
above the bay through the window.
Why is it that at night the world seems so sad
without you beside me my love,
without your reassuring love lying so close,
the simple warmth of touching your skin.
I picked a sprig of jasmine in the dark tonight
walking to the Pizza De Napoli restaurant

glittering on the main drag in town by the water.
Though I stuck the miniature flowers in my buttonhole
they were meant for you.
Now I've placed them in a plastic cup in my blue bedroom
on your small red volume of Pema Chodren's *Awakening Loving-kindness,*
the small red paperback you carried the last couple of years
and presented as gifts to friends and the kids
during the time when compassion and gratitude flowered
within you with such fierce and loving splendor,
like an awesome inner sun blossoming quietly,
like a peony endlessly opening,
determined to reach the top of the sky.
This is your dog-eared copy
that I held in my left hand,
re-reading line by line,
as I held you with all my might
in my shaking right arm
as we danced our magical last dance
as you finally left the floor
we shared with such intensity,
as you had to leave my heart
like this, nowhere,
splintered, aching,
heaving, lost,
a heart on all fours,
a heart knocked down.

The blue-green sea thinks constantly
runs night and day through straits
between two worlds
that never touch.
Swirling currents decide
whether to warm my skin and muscles
or shock me through to the frigid bone,
stun and shake what's left
of my torn will to live.

The sea could not be more joyous at Mykali Beach.
Dylan's *Restless Farewell* in my ears.
But I don't know why sweetheart.
for some reason I see in my mind
the small simple pen drawing I made for you
one afternoon a lifetime ago
when we returned home elated and tired
from a long visit to the Met
(and probably a walk through Central Park)
to catch a show of classic Chinese art.
I sketched in blue pen two glasses filled with wine
with mountains and clouds as background,
and one of those comic old "official" pencils from the City
with "Think and Suggest" printed on the side.
And on the drawing I wrote these words from Ni Tsan in block letters:
We watch the clouds and play with our brushes.
We drink wine and write poems.
The joyous feelings of this day
Will linger after we are parted.
That was over 20 years ago.
I signed the picture: *With Love, Myself, Gary.*
Once during the last month you were here,
on the couch, your glasses on the tip of your nose,
you silently examined your
battered black folder of "special papers."
You showed me the drawing as I read in my rocker.
We both cried and my love I'm weeping now.
So I'll make my stand
And remain as I am
And bid farewell . . .
The Chinese poet's verse
still beats
in time
to my turbulent
constant, struggling,
New York heart.

Gary Zarr

I sigh a lot, blow sea air in and out
to confirm that I am actually still breathing.
We agreed this was paradise
when we visited three years ago.
No matter what comes after this life we said,
floating like kids in the morning,
Paradise cannot be better than this.
I 'm grateful to have made it back
where we both found eternal joy,
sensual and surcharged
in a life that forever counts.
I guess these meandering thoughts
are parts of what's called "the process of mourning,"
a mind unable to fully relish
living here and now,
a heart so pummeled it's unable to truly feel,
a man frantically floundering through memories, dreams and reflections,
stunned and paralyzed by life's sorrows,
thrown from the consolation and adventure of printed pages
and lover's kisses and whisperings in safe shadows.
No matter how I try
I still can't read darling
like during the years we were together.
You were astonished at the doctor's valise stuffed with books
I lugged each day from the library at NYU.
(You smiled and recalled I looked *very intense.*)
Now I listen to music compulsively,
read album liner notes over and over,
travel if I have the courage,
and at the beach stare for hours at the waves, the far off mountains,
the cloudless sky, laughing families in the surf or loud groups in the taverna,
tender couples who seem to always lock in an embrace
once they walk out chest-high on soft sand into the sea.
I step barefoot along a narrow path on this fabulous beach.
The hot pain of the naked stones makes my eyes water.
The sun is vanishing fast.

I found a flat round white stone for you
on Mykali Beach the first morning.
I'm going to bring it back to you dear
and place it on Battle Hill overlooking New York Harbor
under the great beech on the grassy slope
with the headstone I had inscribed
unbelievably
with *your name*
the years *1954* and *2004*.
Yes I will put this stone in my beat-up travel bag
and once home arrange it with other stones I've saved
from the places we traveled on the Open Road,
the heights of Machu Pichu,
the pilgrimage we made before the kids to Walden Pond,
the road through the woods Upstate we walked every season,
the fossil from the sands of Arabia,
wide white shells from "the Stone Beach" at East Marien on the North Fork.
My eyes swim in tears as I write my love
so I can't make out the words too well.
One too many mornings and . . .
Close to me laughing children whack a phosphorescent
lime green tennis ball with bright red paddles.
A mother straightens the bow on a blonde girl's
pink and white bathing suit.
A petite knockout in a hot pink bikini
with her hair pulled up tosses a ball
to a girl who bounces in the incoming waves.
At Mykali I open more and more to waves
of pain, to the realization that you have
sailed away forever *across that lonesome ocean,*
away from me,
in your physical form
for the rest of my life here on planet earth.
Yet I am joyous and deeply grateful for what we had baby,
but horribly choked with sadness
crippled at times, totally unable to figure out
how to keep going,
how to just keep going.

After a swim this morning
I sat on the white stones on shore
the way we did together years ago.
The gentle insistent waves
pushed my chest over and over,
rocked me,
reminded me
that I am nothing
more than a plaything,
a tumbling human pebble
who thinks, laughs, cries, loves,
sings, dreams, fucks,
wanders lost for ages,
who permits the unquestioning ocean
to welcome him home
as only a lonely blue sea can.

A strong swimmer far out at sea
cuts through waves parallel to shore,
stubbornly bobs with each swell,
vanishes for an instant,
then head and shoulders rise
perfectly in line with his destination.
Powerful arms and legs rhythmically
pump in unison,
patiently carry the swimmer
to that special place
where strength and desire are one.
The eternal dialogue
of a determined man
and the vast knowing sea.

How
I wish
you
could
cover
me.
I
struggle
to fall
asleep
again.

You live
more
honestly
when you
have less
and less
to lose.
How
I
want
to hold
you.

The piano swells my ears and then
I read the news today, oh boy,
About a lucky man who made the grade . . .
Hey there original Beatlemaniac
I'm back at Mykali Beach
as I mentioned in other postcards.
A beautiful, chubby serious Upstate girl
grew up in the mountains, found the Fab Four
just in time to fly across the universe.
You began to connect to worlds past The Swamp

across the road and the village green,

to a world stretching in all directions with adventure.

I didn't know what it was all about

but I knew it was something great

was how you put it to me laughing

when you explained last year how you felt

when you bought that wild little book

by John Lennon called *A Spaniard in the Making.*

How this quote captures a vital aspect of you dear,

your electric hunger *to get out there and live*

as fully and widely as possible— *and you did*

with me zooming beside you most of the way

which is why I 'm wounded with guitars playing purple,

crying as the sun bleeds rainbows upon my world.

Sitting on this green and white lounge chair on the beach

I try to cauterize the gigantic volcanic hole

inside me where we used to be mystically attached

freedom, fun and romance rushing back and forth.

I never thought *in a million years* as people say

that I would return to this blessed island alone

by myself all the time— without you, without *you.*

You asked me to set aside grief *after a while*

and to look back upon our life together

with joy, and forward with the same.

My father (gone half my life) met you once and fell for you right away.

In the late 1950s he spoke a testament to his small children

(so much foresight, knowing we all need lifelines,

reasons to go on with this magical and tough game of living)

into his reel-to-reel tape recorder, the first one in the neighborhood.

Under the grapevines, the birds singing, the stone fountain bubbling,

though we were kids, unaware of all the pain and joy in his words,

he proclaimed passionately to us, *To love life is worth anything.*

Yes all we do really need is love baby,

as the hard-edged Beatle knew,

the so-called "pretty," lyrical Liverpool genius does too,

the quiet, spiritual Beatle did,

even the everyman Beatle who bops in time like the rest of us.

Because of you I lucked out, found a passionate world of love,

still possess it now even as I cry for what we once had
because you had to take off so soon,
because you had to gloriously fade away on the gray couch.
(Your stoic heroism unraveled for a few minutes one afternoon
while you wrapped shiny Christmas tree ornaments,
putting them away for the last time with the help of my sister Giulia.
You crumbled, confessed that the worst part of coming to terms
with the fact that you were going to die
was the knowledge
that you were going to leave me
alone for so long
because you knew
I was going to suffer so much.)
As usual you were right my love,
even as I laugh at this crazy life which has left me beaten, senseless,
breathless, hopelessly broken—worthless
in ways beyond belief, so far past anything imaginable,
writhing fleshy shards are what's left,
bits and pieces of what used to be called me,
thrown on the beach,
washing back and forth
in the tender fingertips of an indifferent sea.

Alone at sunset
a small boy and his sister
run and giggle in the wind-rippled waves
on our white stony beach.
If you want to honor my memory
live as fully as I would if I had more years.
Your words overwhelm me.
I go under again, unable to breath,
need to let go, can't hang on anymore,
have to yield to undeniable currents
that pulse through me, over and over,
chanting that you have become a memory,
washing in and out of my mind, my being,
like the waves that hold
what matters in this life,
that have it all
in their inexhaustible transparent hands.

I cried for you again and the moon saw,
swollen and radiant lighting the sea gray.
On my left the cypresses stood still
in silhouette, a damp mist blankets the quiet bay.
Joni Mitchell plays downstairs for our friends.
The world's on fire and last night I couldn't sleep.
The fir trees can't laugh anymore, the birds hide.
When I say your name to the night,
when I slowly say your name to the deep blue dark night,
a cool breeze rushes up into my arms from out of the blackness
from out beyond the lips of the whitewashed balcony.
Nearby in darkness the restless dog's chain clinks.
Far down below the grape vines cannot be seen.
For the night holds every golden human light within its hands,
secrets best left kept inviolate in their little lacquer boxes,
each marked with the date and time of its own special pain.
I know my love as I write it's time to leave
this balcony to open the rickety wooden screen door,
and once again hide in the small blue room
till the faithful morning sun re-lights the world
in ways my fragile heart prays to understand.
Downstairs in the blackness:
Oh I wish I had a river
I could skate away on . . .

Poetry, the hard sharp knife I use to cut into my deepest self, brains to balls
and back again, and again,
to relieve the pressure of this putrescent
unyielding grief, to air out what's left of me,
to scrutinize this Gary-rubbed-raw,
almost not able to be any more,
to listen to John Lennon sing that he's down,
James Brown shout and moan and cry.
Cross-legged and lonely in the dark on the bed,
curled like an animal into a spiral of numbness
I recall last Christmas (your favorite holiday)
you smiled, reclined on the couch, said sweetly,

summing up your journey from childhood pain
to being surrounded and adored by family and friends,
Gary, you know . . . I was always looking for love.
Yes, I realized that darling and we both knew
you found it with the kids and with me, with family, friends.
We held each other tight for as long as we could
and because I had resolved to be your Death Coach
just like I was your Birth Coach when both kids landed magically into our world,
I prepared myself to say: *Okay, watch your breathing . . . Let go . . . Let go . . .*
You're almost there . . . Okay, you're almost there, sweetheart.
Breathe . . . Breathe . . . Great . . . Breathe . . . You're doing great, baby . . .
So I was able to help you to begin that mysterious ultimate flight,
to soar finally and gloriously somewhere I cannot see,
to a place I know you needed to arrive on your own—
this great journey you needed to take without me.
Free as yourself like a butterfly or a great golden bird,
needing to separate your path from mine forever,
decimating loves and lives and dreams and all,
yet seeding this sorrowful and thirsty world with marvels
with flowers, with lightening, and songs and dew.

God is a concept by which we measure our pain . . .
I don't believe in . . .
I don't believe in . . .
Yeah—Jesus, Elvis, Buddha, and even you Johnny.
Do you remember baby
that December day when we had that stunted scraggly lost
naked Christmas tree in our small one-bedroom
in Chelsea and we sat on the mustard-colored Castro convertible
and cried when we heard somebody shot John Lennon,
how we stopped what we were doing— studying
for graduate degrees, working too many jobs
to make ends meet but so happy and in love,
and we wept together as the needles
rained from the already-dry branches
tinkling sadly one by one like cosmic tear drops
onto the plastic white floor cover you bought at the corner drugstore.

Gary Zarr

I slump into this memory darling,
all about losing you forever,
how you fell from this world like one of those pine needles
for some reason unable to attach any longer.
And I will fall too one day at some preordained moment,
in some specific place that patiently waits for me alone.
Perhaps my hands like treasured doves protected like yours in my final moments,
my arms and face stroked and kissed by lovers and friends and family,
or else maybe I'll split alone or surrounded by clouds of mysterious strangers
who have no idea who I was, what I did, what I tried and failed to do.
But no matter what comes I realize I will really never leave
this world of marvels alone because you will cheer me on,
wait for me, inexplicably and inevitably, as I descend
like one of those lost little Christmas tree needles
that matured in an unknowable smoky-breath forest up North
and at a precise instant just had to let go one day,
couldn't hold on any longer, shouldn't perhaps, didn't need to any more,
even though the tree had found such a warm safe home
inside out of the cold, celebrated and cherished if only for a season.
A small tree rescued
from a frigid, foreign, frenetic,
blinking neon-lit New York street
in holiday time.
The dream is over.
What more can I say?

Very early one morning I took a long walk up the mountain overlooking Samos
Town; a couple of hours later, I was back at the Fat Guy's Café.

Hey there baby—very early morning walk to Upper Vathi.
I climbed narrow winding streets.
Surprised cats bathed in the fresh light.
Old women silent on balconies, workmen hammered
plaster from the walls of white gem box houses
with green and blue trim, quiet just after dawn.
Clusters of homes and shops nest like cubist doves in Monmartre,
interconnected white and pastel human cubes

with profusions of flowers and caged birds singing.
An old man smiled when I wished him
good morning as he stepped out his front door.
No cars, the vegetable market vendors setting up.
Walking without speaking in the serene morning,
I heard an alarm clock go off in one of the homes
built within an arm's reach of each other.
(Designed to create a labyrinth to confuse invaders, Russ explained.)
I was so close to the sleeper I felt like I was in the bedroom myself.
I wander new streets
like we always did, byways we never knew existed,
the jasmine-scented just-after-sunrise time,
climbing, climbing, accompanied only by the sound
of my footsteps all the way to the white church on the mountain top.
Below a solitary white boat floated in the dark blue harbor.
All this washes through my mind as I sit here
back in the Fat Guy's Café as the old men shoot the breeze,
at the end of a memorable solo walk
at the time of day you taught me to cherish,
when the world wakes with joy and surprise,
though now I am loaded with grief sweetheart,
with this sweet sadness that sinks like a disintegrating sugar cube
into the dark swirls of the wide open coffee cup of my life.

Quiet, one afternoon home after shopping for provisions for dinner, I sat on
the terrace of Russ and Laura's place, and I became a captive of the Aegean
again; the sea possessed me and I tumbled into a reverie and conversation with
my lost friend. Again, she had to know, and I had to explain everything to her.
Face it, those first months after she died, I had no one to talk to, like the way
we spoke, all the time and about everything. I had no one to talk to, really talk
to, like that. Maybe, I didn't want to, couldn't.

While I had coffee early this morning by myself on the terrace
seven white doves shot right at me
from the darkness of the immense cypresses next door
like a Japanese print come suddenly to supersonic life.
Streaking past the tall pines facing the quiet bay

they soared past, dived wildly, flapping their wings
cawing in a strange, intentional way.
Then they dramatically climbed, further— and vanished.
And the fresh world was once again still and awakening.
A magic lightening moment "out of nowhere" as we would say.
How you would have enjoyed this show darling.
(I can visualize your gray-blue eyes, the color of the Aegean,
wide with spirals of wonder as I write to you what happened.)
I know it sounds strange but I am sure you would appreciate
this fabulous morning vision and that you would *get it*—
this miraculous gift of sanity and splendor that came to me,
that was given to my life movie for some reason.

I like the pocket-size Museum Café near the outdoor fruit and vegetable market
where just a couple of years ago we shopped in the narrow park
that used to have the giant bird cages Laura painted long ago in Chelsea.
This morning I learned to say *celery*, *potatoes* and *carrots* in Greek
and I bought vegetables for Russ' famous fish soup.
We ate the heavy, friendly fish we bought yesterday morning
and greens, French fries, a Greek salad—fresh with clear olive oil.
Had our trip worked out three years ago, I know you would have cooked
up a joyous storm here with Russ and Laura in the kitchen
where they spend all their time with guests.
(It's the only room in their unique, profound house *with chairs*— that's so cool, right?)
The kids, so much younger back then, would have had the run of the place,
played with the two mother cats outside and their kittens,
raced around the stone-walled terraces, splashed and laughed at Mykali Beach.
Instead love, I have returned to paradise to explore
a black pain blended into a timeless beauty that has attracted
pilgrims as far back as the ancient world streaming to the Temple of Hera.
I guess this aching validates our life of inspiration together.
The moon which hangs outside the windows of my little blue bedroom,
should be full and glowing and voluptuous tonight
through the waving pines and cypress silhouettes,
like a suspended smiling peach ready to be devoured juice and all.
When I sit with Russ and Laura on the terrace each day at sunset we sip Scotch,
talk in the soft voices of early evening, the sounds of night coming on.

I carry your little red Pema Chodron book with me on walks.
I reread a chapter in the Museum Café earlier today,
recheck your written comments— blue ink stars
and underlined passages that hit home.
I understand even more that the last year or so of your time with us,
you were opening, continually opening, like a gloriously expanding peony
until finally, petals liberated, you stretched beyond where we can see,
to become one with everything around us— all that there is—
even these tough old palm trees here in the park, the deep blue bay in front of me,
even reaching as far as the shivering clear water at the bottom of the fountain basin
in the Museum Café where I sit alone.
I feel very calm, sweetheart, maybe this means "at peace."
Tomorrow is the six-month anniversary since you took off.
In flashes I begin to glimpse a way to go on living
though it's such a long walk back home.

On the sand at the beach, in the sea, I wrestled with her death, with death
itself, tried to imagine how it goes, how death goes, to understand what my love
had experienced, where she had gone, ahead of me, ahead of you reading these
words wherever you are in the world at this moment never to be repeated.

The smooth white stone that claimed me in this poems sits on my desk, a small
battered blonde wooden desk I had pushed back home on a dolly for Gail one
autumn as a surprise gift from a used office furniture store in Chelsea. I cherish
and protect the white stone, which soothes me in a strange way; my giant
white worry bead straight from the ocean, from the earth, from the heart of
losing her.

The water is crystalline today warm and very quiet.
We swam in the late morning and I sat on the stones,
watched tiny white fish, translucent with black bands on their delicate tails,
swim around my submerged torso.
I found myself rubbing a round white stone
underwater with my right hand thinking that perhaps
dying is really like floating on your back both ears under water,
the world more and more cushioned in submarine sounds,
not able to understand anymore what's happening,

and what you're able to see is undulating and super vivid.
Your own heart beat (or is it someone else's or the universe's?)
reverberates throughout your being.
Maybe it's like being slowly submerged like an immense fish,
in a strange yet recognizable submarine world of dreams, visions, feelings,
the faces you love, the sky, a cozy familiar room, colors, sounds, experiences,
your life becomes borderless, slow, hazy, just swirling snatches of real life movies,
transformed into brilliant colors like a Matisse collage come alive,
that floats gradually away, further and further and further,
until you twist and struggle perhaps, but just to get comfortable,
to reach a point where you no longer know or care about
struggling and holding on to even what you love most,
you give up trying not to drown, fight that impulse, quiet completely,
like when you learn to swim and have to let the water carry you.
Maybe dying is just a question of faith and daring like learning to ride a bike,
death like a bike we have to hop on and on the ride shout with laugher and joy
no matter how terrifying it seems because we know it is the ultimate ride of a lifetime.
And then maybe all of a sudden you're not under water anymore,
but finally free, totally free for the first time, rushing out into the universe,
experiencing what has no name and is beyond fear and love and expression.
Maybe, maybe, maybe this is what occurs dear when our life is completed,
what happened to you as we held your hands, we stroked your arms,
kissed your face and all of us repeated how much we loved you,
as you laid on the couch like a fairy tale queen with the family
and even our wise cat Fellini (you called him, *Our little friend)*
surrounding you, launching you with absolute love
upon the unknowable sea on your flight to far-off marvelous summits.
These thoughts and images and many more flowed through me
as I compulsively rubbed the white palm-sized stone in the sea
which had selected my hand to touch with its message
like God fingering poor Adam on the Sistine Chapel ceiling,
an image we saw together many times with the jostling rest of the world.
The sun cleansed me as I held the stone.
Our friends bobbed like happy kids engaged in serious play with the waves.
Families enjoyed their day at the beach.
I realized that I was crying again,
directly this time, straight into the immortal sea.

One afternoon, I met huge Yannis Scopos, the proprietor of the taverna I visited every day Mykali Beach. Gail would have loved him— you reading these words, too. Over time, I felt deeply connected to Yannis and his small, feisty, cheerful Australian wife Karen, who seemed to do most of the work in their restaurant. We really didn't say much to each other, as I reflect upon the length of our brief conversations. Yet I was bound to them.

Yannis and Karen became important parts of my inner journey, as I searched for ways to go on living, and to sort out the remnants of me. Hidden under my shades and baseball cap, it was a veritable weep-a-thon; tears came in gusts and unannounced. (When I got back to New York after the first trip I told friends that I would write a book called *The Joy of Crying*. A sure fire best seller. I was half kidding. I had spent most of my life laughing, and now I was making up for it with a vengeance; and I was getting good at crying, I realized).

We are never shown the proper and most effective ways to cry or laugh. What we need to know most, we are never taught. But then life steps in from time to time and takes over, we go on life auto pilot, and if we pay enough attention, life itself teaches us how to be human, more deeply a man, a more expansive, enriched woman— and this comes about because of the showers of tears, of joy, enormous sorrow.

Yanis Scopos, the huge guy with tattoos who runs the Mykali Taverna Scopos
where I come each day to commune with you,
to eat, drink too much wine and beer, write a bit, listen to James Brown,
Lucinda Williams, Reverend Gary Davis, Glenn Gould, Clapton, Jimmy
Rogers, Chopin, Fela, Dvorak, the Stones, Mendelssohn, Sarah Vaughn, Woody
Guthrie, Orchestre Baobab, Brahms, Tony Bennett, Leonard Bernstein
apparently likes me enough to send me a carafe of white wine.
I like that guy, he confides to Russ, who cries,
This is a special guy!
Only the best for him!
This is a special guy!
I'm touched baby by how our friends are taking care of me.
I was right to choose this journey back to paradise to explore
the great wound that crisscrosses my body and spirit.
What are we going to do when you leave? Russ bellows at the table.

I'll be back, don't worry.
Good, good.
Bravo. Bravo.
Of course you will be here too, whenever I return,
if I am able to come back at all,
but you know that, no need to explain.
I mean how could I venture so far from home
without my great Traveling Buddy?
I'm feeling terrible again as I write these words to you,
from my floundering, turbulent flight in search of refuge.
I am crying again sweetie.
Sorry, but I miss you so much.
And you're saying I know,
Come on now, Gary.
Enough with being gloomy.
Come on—let's get going! Come on now baby.
I 'm trying to hold on, but I'm lost again.
Confused, I can't see.

Bruce Chatwin, a writer I admire, came into my mind at the beach one
afternoon, and I recalled his description of visiting the dying Noel Coward,
another favorite, a writer of delightful, cutting insights but also of deep
poignancy and longing.

He must have been suffering at the dinner table,
the dying Noel Coward,
stoned from the drugs
floating
on streams of tireless worldly wit.
The young Bruce Chatwin ate lunch in Coward's Caribbean home.
The Master's last words to his student, also gone from this world:
Don't let anything artistic stand in your way.

Diving and floating in the water, I continued to speak to my lost country girl
from up north, and music and images and ideas swirled in and out of my mind
with the cold and warm currents of the rushing water between Greece and
Turkey.

I swim in the Aegean wearing my Yankee cap.
You would be amused by this I know,
smile at me from shore or floating nearby,
anticipate how I will regale friends back home
with tales of how the dark blue cap was baptized
in the sacred water of the Mediterranean
that rushes cold and hot between two worlds.
Close to you I will always stay . . .
The Chairman of the Board croons . . .
. . . though you're far away . . .
An overwrought Scandinavian couple bounces and laughs
in the crystal blue green sea . . .
Wherever you go, my heart will go too
What can I do?
I only want to be close to you.
Violins now with Frank, the persistent slapping surf, kids squeal.
The afternoon wind picks up, runs through my hair.
I notice that many young couples visiting paradise
are *so serious*, I guess trying out what it means to live together,
more or less happy and at ease with each other.
Somehow at that stage we seemed (or am I just getting what's called old?)
so much more lighthearted, always planning days of adventure,
laughing, never bickering, passionately talking about
what we just read, what was in the news, planning new ways to live.
But maybe that's just my constant current of sorrow
lighting my bewildered mind with killer flashes like in a storm Upstate at night.
PS: Baby I could swear Maria Callas swam by me today.
I read somewhere that she had her lyrical ashes of passion
sprinkled into the Aegean with the rest of what we know
and will never understand as mortals journeying on this earth.

My painter friends are wonderful chefs. I will always be grateful that they
shared their paradise with me— no questions asked, or even thought of. I have
known Russ and Laura for 30 years, since way before the kids were born. We
met when Gail and I, not yet married, blissful, juggling jobs and graduate
classes, lived next door to Russ and Laura in a cozy one-bedroom in Chelsea
on 21st Street and 7th Avenue. Like all truly close friends, Russ and Laura are

family, no actually better, because they are one step removed—they have been selected to be in my life, because of a soulful kinship, an ineffable bond that doesn't need to be explained, that just is.

The first journey to Samos was ending, but I still obsessively needed to explain my experiences to Gail, my daily routine—the healing Mediterranean, the scene at the taverna, conversations with Yannis and our painter friends—.in celestial postcards. As my flight home approached, it became more pressing and urgent that I get everything down in these shaggy, poetic postcards, so she would know, just so she would know.

I'm at the back end of the main square by the harbor
in the Fat Guy's Café marveling at the two tubby
dainty pink brothers who run this wonderful place.
Their mother's consigned to the kitchen— where else?
And the father, the small old guy, slouched with his cronies,
grins at a corner table, watching the world go by.
I bought lemons, beets (*bazaria* in Greek), and greens (*horta*)
for dinner tonight, also a couple of bottles of a red Greek wine
which the three of us have zeroed in on as our favorite.
(You would like it— it's smooth and full-bodied.)
Last night I conceded to Russ on the music front,
and Bach's *Partitas*, which are part of me,
resounded through the old white house,
clear across the street, down over the houses and out to sea.
Our main course was Russ' superb fish soup (it has the same
stock we drank in fish soup in Spain, Italy, and the Middle East),
ate dishes of sautéed greens with olive oil and lemon juice,
fresh tomatoes and feta cheese, and we talked
for hours, and were silent together too.
I am well packed with tacky, over-the-top gifts to bring back home—
only one more to get— a t-shirt for Danny— after this cappuccino.
I'll try to pick up the two Greek papers (*The News* and *The Free Press*)
Russ wants at the newsstand at the edge of the square.
(A short, leathery guy with a cigarette dangling
from his parched thin lips pops up and disappears in the newsstand kiosk.

Why do all these news guys around the world all look like neighborhood bookies?
Answer: Because they usually are.)
Fueled by wine and fresh bad news in the papers,
evenings we continue to rail in our semi-informed passionate way,
about how *the world is going to hell in a hand basket*, as Russ repeats.
It's bad kid, don't kid yourself, it's really bad.
And it's getting worse, Russ intones like a sage
in a Greek tragedy that must turn comic because
this is *now*—and tragedy died long ago
when the purity of life slipped through our hands somehow.
Each morning at 8 AM sharp Russ turns on a dusty
monster old boom box to listen to the BBC World News.
(Remember all the places around the world we heard Big Ben baby?)
But all that comes out of the radio is a steady Phil Spector wall of sound
bombardment of grating static that rattles the dishes and makes even
the starving feral cats outside the door dance back.
Laura rolls her eyes as we drink the hot coffee Russ makes
without fail every morning as he whistles and waits
for us to finally wake (Russ still stays up half the night
reading, sitting at the kitchen table, turning life over, kneading it).
Yesterday for the first time I emerged from my Garbo-like silence
at the Mykali Beach Taverna Scopos.
I spoke to the mountainous smiling tattooed Yanis Scopos
who runs the place with his sweet worldly Australian wife Karen.
Yanis' parents own the land under the restaurant.
A bear of a man, he's a middle-aged hippie I guess,
Indian chiefs tattooed on his arms and
a small dark blue peace sign drawn on the top of one hand.
(This morning I saw Yanis for the first time in town and not at his café
shooting the breeze with a friend on the steps of the wine store.
We shook hands and I said I would see him later at the beach.
Walking back to the Fat Guy's Café I saw him a second time.
Yanis seemed late for an appointment and hustled across the square.
But he stopped for a moment to point in the direction of the liquor store,
and then he laughed and shouted in English, *That is your favorite store!*)
Apparently Yanis just cut his legendary pony tail
which Karen said dryly, *used to reach all the way to his arse.*

You have a sympathetic face, Yanis sitting said to me
smiling his skin dark and almost blue-colored.
He finished a huge mug of beer as I stood waiting for a taxi
to take me over the tawny hills of Samos back home
to Russ and Laura's neighborhood called Kalami (bamboo).
I had chatted with Karen a couple of times on previous days.
She said she liked music and that Yanis did too and that
he used to be a DJ in Athens so they agreed to switch off
the sad Greek love songs on their sound system
and instead play a CD I lent them of Eric Clapton doing Robert Johnson.
My wife told me, Yanis said soberly referring to your death darling.
I think everyone has bad things— everyone.
Yanis pulled on a cigarette and narrowed his eyes to slits.
But we have to go on with life.
I Got a Sweet Hearted Woman played, the waves splashed close by.
Life is not happy— we have happy moments.
We have to go on with life. We take the joy and go on.
I nodded, standing beside Yannis.
I am here to be reborn, I replied.
Bravo. Good.
Then Yanis' gargantuan timeless head beamed like Buddha.
His mammoth belly and chest rolled with approval under a worn orange t-shirt.
I'm writing in such detail my love so that you get the flavor
of my last few days in paradise this time round,
the paradise we shared with lucidity and with passion,
with such a natural ease that has no beginning, has no end.

It's morning as I write and when I get back to Russ and Laura's house
(I catch a cab at the taxi stand in the square)
we'll all get ready to go the beach— for the last time.
The usual routine goes like this: We arrive at Mykali Beach, we swim,
I claim a lounge chair with my towel and pile on a couple of stones to fight the winds.
In the café I have a bite to eat, Russ has an iced beer with me and Laura has coffee.
Then our friends go back home, I finish my lunch, and re-take my chair.
I listen to music, walk into the sea a few times, think about you,
listen to more music, cry, laugh softly sometimes, watch the bathers,
wonder what you and I would be doing, what would have been in store for us

if you hadn't been mysteriously taken away,
and between waves, I ceaselessly write these postcards to you dear.
While on Samos, I've dipped into an old copy of *The Greek Way*,
and a small rose-colored copy of Lao Tzu.
(The *Tao* was the first book I ever gave you, remember?
It was winter break senior year.
My slender white paperback Wytter Bynner translation.
After you went Upstate for the Christmas holidays with my little book gift
you vainly tried to decipher my signature.
That was the year your beloved grandfather Loren died.
Later you told me that Lao Tzu helped get you through that sad time.)
I'm ready to head home to New York— to the kids, family, friends,
the zooming life back there, knowing as we both said,
that life is constant transformation with both joy and sorrow in every life.
The soft morning breeze arrives from the deep blue-green water by the port.
A large ferry with a dolphin painted on its smokestack sails away.
Jasmine-scented Samos, a major center of the ancient world,
home of Pythagoras, the fabled Temple of Hera,
one of the wonders of the old world.
I know that I will still get to rummage one final time
through the tchotchkes in the tourist shop on the other side of the square,
in search of the tackiest Samos t-shirt I can find.
And once the newspapers arrive at the bookie's newsstand,
there'll be the death-defying taxi ride uphill, in and out of the narrow walled streets,
up to the rambling white house with the creaking high metal front gate
where I have found refuge, moments of peace,
laughter and conversation, beauty and mystery,
a place out of time, to begin to understand
where I painfully stand.
Wish you here baby. But you know that.

On the last trip to Mykali Beach, Laura and Russ spoke about the colors of the
sea, about how hard it is to paint. We stood in the water as we talked, floated
in the waves not far from each other in case we had something important to
say. Like happy children, we rolled with the Aegean, but then doesn't everyone
become a child, small and open and yearning, in the sea.

There is something about the sea today, Laura said quietly.
Soft, warm, blue gray waves caressed us.
We ate sausages and French fries with beer.
I wonder if the sea comes from where you are my love,
somewhere from the shimmering edge of blue infinity.
It's hard to paint the horizon line there, Gary—
the edge of the sea and sun, that point of infinity,
Laura explained as Russ nodded seriously.
Both have spent their lives trying, I thought,
as I stood up to my neck in the water and watched our two painter friends
swim like children, bobbing and backstroking in the blues.
When you see it, you have the sun— the sun.
But when you try to paint it, you only have color,
so you have to solve that problem.
And then Laura smiled, almost embarrassed
to be speaking so directly about the infinite,
how we seek to capture it, art,
mind after mind, heart after heart,
hands following hands, everywhere, and throughout time,
using the colorful bottles of our own making,
the strange way we seem to stumble upon the eternal,
out there on the edge of the Mediterranean,
or find it crouching under tangled grapevines,
radiating from flaming hibiscus, brooding by roadside diners,
in garbage tossed into battered dumpsters,
in how the bay purrs and birds sing as sunset arrives,
how the faithful sun decides to return each day
no matter what we have done, no matter what crimes we have committed.
Tomorrow another plane will soar away from paradise
with passengers intent upon roads without end.
But I know that the endless resides here
at the intersection of these far away blues.

I wrote this poem standing on the circular white balcony outside my small blue
room. I didn't look or feel the same; I had been transformed over the two weeks
I had been on the magic island.

My skin is brilliantly lit a golden it hasn't been for ages.
The sea shouts a bluish-green reminder towards Mykali Taverna.
Life is the four elements and five senses, Russ declared today.
Bamboo swings in soft wind with an easy beat.
Stubby pine moves quicker, firs with a slow sensuality.
When the ravens and swallows call it a day at sunset
bats as big as sparrows shoot and dart against the night glow.
There are still stars enough and dreams enough my love
to cast rainbows of glory and unvanquished splendor
upon our yearning hearts and restless souls,
to beat this world with drums and cymbals
meant to be heard by the heavenly moon itself,
by those flocks of ranging, luminescent, godforsaken joyous stars,
dancing lost in my forever eyes.

The Greek waiter in Scopos Taverna was a dead ringer for a classical young male Greek sculpture, the famous *kouros*. What made this realization so powerful was the young guy's total naturalness, his incomprehension of his own timeless beauty. Cavafy, the great Greek poet, came to mind one afternoon as I ate lunch. I am sure the spirit of that proper Greek poet from Alexandria, a devoted historian yet an abiding sensualist, hovered nearby.

Horny, refined Cavafy would dig the waiter here,
would've composed breathless odes with great precision
to honor this young guy's unconscious beauty,
literally the embodiment of the classic Greek *kouros* statues
on view in the small Samos Museum off the square by the market.
Languid, round, down-turned lips, seemingly unintentionally
pouting like Elvis the King, broad angular shoulders, narrow waist.
He stands taking orders from a German couple
with the sensual tilt of his hips like Michelangelo's *David*.
Thoughtless, serious, barely smiling, such purity.
I learned yesterday that he is studying to be a plumber,
or is it a mechanic, just a local kid supported
by his parents working in the taverna this summer.
How could he ever know who he really is I wonder,
as he moves like a huge cat in his running shoes.

How splendid that my waiter here in paradise
is a living sculpture, marble yet pliable and alive,
his millions of cells unaware and replicating
the urgent, passionate classical genetic messages drifting
across millennia from the depths of the wine dark sea.

The sea and sun were my physicians— Samos, my spa and sanatorium.

I float and so my feet stand on solid ground.
I cry and I so I laugh madly.
I wonder constantly so waves of certainty slap my face.
I deeply kiss life's oracular lips so I am gloriously alone.
Sitting under the blanket of stars by the sea
in my silence I speak to every starry world there is.
My non-stop dreaming makes life so real.
The further I reach for you, the nearer you are.
The closer you are my love, the more I'm lost.

The sun is a scalpel
that makes me whimper
like a beaten dog
on the lounge chair at the beach.
Undeniable light explores
every dark crevice
of my bitter heart's
wondrous memories,
its restless, tremulous yearning.

So long, how I hate to see you go.
So long, how I hate to see you go.
And the way that I will miss you baby
I guess you will never know.
We've been together so long
To have to separate this way.
We've been together so long
To have to separate this way.
I'm gonna let you go head on now baby

Pray that you'll come back home some day . . .
in my ears and night arrives again.
Soon I'll have my last whiskey during our famous cocktail hour
on the terrace in our friends' kingdom
of only authentic acts with the pistachio tree limb
that hangs too low and if you're not careful drips sap on your head
when you enter through the creaky high rusting dark green iron gate.
Soon I'll leave paradise missing you as much,
knowing that our time worked out just right,
like when we first got to know each other,
making love in the afternoon in your apartment on West 13th Street,
listening to Louis Armstrong, Bach's lute music,
sweating so happy, lying on our backs in your bedroom,
just as small but much happier than pale blue room on Samos.
When we broke the bed on 23rd Street the people
in the courtyard below mimicked our cries and moans.
In my studio off 8th Avenue the Puerto Rican guy
next door used to play his electric organ and sing along
as we laughed and made love on my used Castro sofa bed.
(It weighed a ton—how many places did we lug it?)
I keep reminding myself that life's still here baby,
that we shared paradise as long as we could,
that it's all okay and I know it inside me—that it is really all okay.
So see you soon sweetheart.
Got you something special from my trip,
something really cool, wild and fun,
something you'll get a kick out of.

Russ found a wiry, strong Yugoslavian laborer named Georgas to fix a section of the stone wall that had collapsed behind the house near the abandoned well and great walnut tree. In the old days, Russ would have done the work himself, but he hires workers now instead of showing off his expert skill at house painting, masonry and wood work. That's behind him; grudgingly, he has learned to let life go it a bit, to loosen the reins of his intense drive to live on his own terms and in all ways, to demonstrate his force to the world.

Georgas was also going to white wash the house. These were chores Russ had done religiously each summer for decades when he opened the house, usually arriving a month before Laura finished the school year, working as an art teacher in New York. Russ literally built the walls around the gardens, chairs, tables, stone stairs— and of course, the frames of all his paintings. He is a craftsman as well as a painter and his hands have the honored, weathered look of a field hand, a shoemaker, a common laborer. Though one of the most well read men, Russ' rough hands, and tough, direct voice and manner, belie a gentle and sensitive artistic, iconoclastic soul, a man devoted to the classical Greek virtues— the true, the beautiful and the good— and freedom, freedom at any cost, independence, the fiery Greek oracle of free thinking and free expression.

The steady work of Georgas and the pounding of his hammer became the timeless, workman's music that ended my first trip to Samos after her death. By that time, all the cabbies on the island, who drove manically around hair pin turns and up and down mountainsides, honking their horns on blind turns, had earned nicknames. I knew many of their stories as my trip to paradise eased into something else, the resumption of my life in "the real world," no, my world, the world of "the new norm," my life back in New York.

As light comes I hear the hammer crash against huge stones in the yard.
The earth absorbs the full force and sound of Georgas,
the sinewy dark Albanian worker repairing the stone retaining wall
along the white-washed terrace near the great walnut tree.
From time to time the tinny sound of his heavy shovel
scraping against rocks embedded in the earth for centuries
floats up to me as I sit on the white terrace
outside my pale blue room overlooking the bay.
I leave for the airport in two hours,
picked up by a taxi driver I nicknamed Dean Martin
because his squinting, laughing eyes and ruddy complexion
exude the perfect TV boozy nonchalance of old Dino.
It seems that my local Dean Martin has a son
who also drives taxi on Samos, but he's unsmiling and intense,
all business and from what I'm told he's so quiet
because he is a newlywed and exhausted from lovemaking.

Last night on the lower terrace at sunset
Russ picked me fresh almonds from a tree in the front yard
and I chewed the sweet soft nuts with my whiskey.
The moon rose over a world of a thousand greens and tender breezes.
When I left Mykali Beach yesterday for the last time
Karen gave me a beer on the house while I waited for a cab.
She called to Yanis who was working in the back handling fish.
I wasn't able to spend much time with him since
Dean Martin's apparently fatigued son was speeding to the taverna.
So I downed my complimentary iced mug and got ready to share the cab
with an older Scandinavian couple who have a home on Samos.
Come again, come next year, Karen said.
I kissed her and pumped Yanis' enormous hand with my two.
Then I rushed with my canvas museum beach bag to the gray taxi.
Listen to this baby— yesterday when I returned to the taverna
from the beach the place was empty as usual which was fine with me.
Karen wiped down a table, the cats (there must a dozen)
lounged out in the open and when she saw me,
Karen said warmly, *Hey, here he comes— Mr. Paradise.*
Not a bad name, right baby? *Mr. Paradise.*
Maybe it means I've been able to devour what I've smelled, tasted,
touched, heard and seen here these last two weeks,
tried to digest the final stages of our journey together.
Now, as I write to you, the mist burns off;
the deep blue sea this morning runs northwest.
The rooster next door crows, another far away answers, the birds sing in their trees.
The pair of dark towering cypresses I've studied for two weeks
stand vigil, dance and smile in warm, smooth ocean breezes
for every pilgrim who passes this way in search of soothing and peace.

I wrote a song on the plane back to New York. I imagine the last part as lyrics
married to soulful Cuban music; maybe some day they will find their mate.

The traveling moon was soft last night.
The sea wind cooled my chest and face.
The cypresses lifted me to starry jasmine heights
on the terrace by my small pale blue room all alone.

And now I'm flying on Air France over the Mediterranean
out over Florence and then on to Paris,
dancing inside to a sexy, sad *danzon* sung by the *Buena Vista Social Club*.
You're here I see so clearly and we two Age of Aquarians
twirl and slide and leap just like old Fred and Ginger
over shimmering seas and constellations of magical islands.
And we're laughing my love! We're laughing again!
We're holding hands as we tilt and swoop and soar,
having the time of our lives with the world at our feet.
I could write such sweet sad *boleros* for you darling,
like *Dos Gardenias*, exactly like those sorrowful flowers,
playing in my ears as I rush from one world to the next.
Each day I could write you such wild ecstatic love-soaked songs
like the fiery, delirious *Candela* to you my lost love,
with lines like these sung by a vigorous
melancholy dreamy razzle-dazzle man:
About your peony face like the sun itself
About your peony face like the sun itself
Your deep gray sea blue eyes
Those deep gray sea blue eyes
Your smile with the fresh morning sun
Your smile with the fresh morning sun
Your shy soft skin in warm shadows
Your shy soft skin in warm shadows
The music plays in my head my love
The music plays in my bed my love
Yeah, yeah, yeah. Wow, wow, wow.
Spanish guitars groove as my heart beats
Spanish guitars groove as my heart beats
I fly over clouds to you my love
I fly over mountains to you my love
Come, let's dance this night away!
Come, let's dance this night away!
From sacred Samos to Paris
And then back to New York again
Till we're home, till we're home again
I'll leave off now, sweet,

Cause I'll see you soon
I'll leave off for now, love,
Cause I'll see you soon
How is it possible?
How is it so real?
A love that is life itself,
A life that will never end
I am lost in you, I am found in you
I am lost in you, I am found in you
I cry for you and I laugh wildly for you
I cry for you and I laugh madly for you
What more can I say my woman of purple dolphins
Golden woman who was my muse and my inspiration
Yeah, yeah, yeah. Now, now, now.
Let's dance! Let's dance!
Let's kiss! Let's kiss!
The guitars sing, a trumpet moans, maracas hiss
How I adore you
How I adore you
How I adore you
These are the words I hear
These are the words I hear
These are the words right now
These are the words right now
And they will live forever
And they will live forever
And they will live forever

II Returning

> *Words are flowing out*
> *Like endless rain into a paper cup.*
> *They slither while they pass*
> *They slip away across the universe.*
> *Pools of sorrow, waves of joy*
> *Are drifting through my open mind*
> *Possessing and caressing me . . .*
> *Across the Universe*
> Lennon-McCartney

Four summers later I returned to Samos. By this time my river of grief flowed mostly within, invisible to others, yet still powerful and undeniable. By the second trip, as it does even now, my rushing river of grief continued to water the deep underground lakes and springs of me, giving life to the cooing, clacking, hooting, roaring, flapping, teeming marshes and forests and jungles of me out in the world.

The *Gary* that is seen and known actually exists only because of the undying, mysterious love, the nurturing, urgent yet soothing uprising flow from the underground, unseeable lakes that faithfully feed my river of grief. Without this river of sorrow, I would have died of thirst, a lover's thirst, for his beloved, lost forever in this desert we call the world.

The furious internal currents of my river of grief, which made it virtually impossible for me to settle down on the first trip, had subsided. I had been severely wounded, and I had the scars to prove it. But I was making forays into love, to try to experience life, the vast range of it, again. I actually was able to be with my friends Russ and Laura. I was capable of staying with them, and what was in front of me— Mykali Beach, the Fat Guy's Café, Scopos Taverna, the trees and gardens and grapevines at the house.

During my second journey to Samos I was able to fully focus on Russ and Laura in ways I couldn't during my first trip. I paid attention to them, and they emerge more in these poems. I was able to better see what was around me. I was able to be *present*; and I was even strong enough to *imagine* other times and places beyond just me. I was in the world again, not just regarding what passed outside me like a man who had landed from outer space.

But my life will forever be anchored to her, to Gail, to us together, given deep meaning and context because she had existed at all, and luckily been part of my life. My story intertwined with Gail gives meaning, shadow and dimensions and depth to my world; it roots me and drives me forward.

But nothing present or to come in my life is diminished by this fact, believe me, and all loves are ecstatic and real and unique and precious and treasured and welcome. For love alone makes us complete, love helps us to become fully human. Love affirms our short time on this planet, our residence here, as a great poet wrote. Because of the loss of Gail, a catastrophic turning point for me, a life lesson of profound meaning and implications, I am able to better appreciate the world around me. I learned so much from her life and her leaving, from our merry and brilliant time together, not that I needed the lesson, about me, about others.

You do get up, you rise like a prizefighter, you stand once more, and then you awaken as after a long illness or stretch of captivity, and you begin to take your first baby steps into a new world, your new world of being, without that one, your special person.

And all of this is truly freeing. This breaking through and away from the past, which no matter what we believe, is just an idea, just in our mind, though it is real and immensely strong and also, if you have been fortunate, fabulously rich and sweet with adventure and love and union.

If you are honest enough, and courageous, and to some degree foolish and heedless, you dive right into your own special river of grief, and though you think you will drown many times, you pop up time after time into fresh air, and you find yourself in strange new, marvelous places. Grief wants to carry you to joy if you let it, to redemption, to awareness, but you can't always see this, because most times you are confused and lost and drifting. But grief, even when it is most fresh and paralyzing, wants to make you whole again. That's why it cuts you down with such precision and coldness like wild wavy grass that needs mowing. Grief, even at its most deadly, is a way of healing.

But this takes time—you have to make the doleful and exhilarating journeys to paradise in order to come out the other side.

Something else happens too, many things really, some of which are expressed, or partially so, here. Life happens, continues to, quietly and undeniably, without marching bands and glaring lights, simply, gradually, day by day, the way nature renews itself with each fresh dawn.

Life happens, you happen with it, parts of it, and you are reborn, even though your lover, as you knew her or him, is gone forever, for all time as we know it here on planet earth.
There is a way out, into life again, into love again. There is, but you have to earn it, find it, cherish it, know it and name it.

With my friends, on my second pilgrimage to Samos, I tried to—I did.

Straight from the heart shoots my love of this world, explosions of bliss, kisses and tormented cries.
Now I know
more.
Now I know
more.
Sleepless life work always in progress.
Dreams like geese paired for life
fly to distant mountains.
We must love as we can
past horrors and choked-off lives.
You taught me this
or life did mysteriously
ripped apart my fine-tuned workman's heart strings
transformed them into bloody rainbows triple strung
beating, crimson, purplish radiant yellow aching.

No more flurries of scrawled postcards.
Not like before, not so many,
trips to get stamps at post offices and candy stores.
No more
postcards like before.
Emails now, faster, rocketing direct
invisible like light
like love, like our lives.
Now old school postcards just get stuck to refrigerators,
pinned to walls, tucked between pages
to mark how far we've gotten in the story.
So I'll send you emails from now on sweetheart
though I'll pick up postcards too
because the shiny photos say so much.
I'm assuming you have a fridge and books
for them where you are my love.

Laura wants to see
what I wrote for you four years ago.
Russ too, I know.
I carry my first batch of postcards in my backpack.
James Taylor sings "Handyman,"
gentle, consoling, way-back-then music.
I'm so rooted to *now*
like before but renewed,
still a work in progress.
Heart overflows, eyes clear most times,
tongue works, rest of me too in overdrive,
still reaching to touch,
open and ready for more life.
Two hours till I fly,
eyes hyper wide and waiting for take-off.
Even after so much battering and joy
this boy-man-me-rolled-into-a-single-Gary
remains intent upon playing one more day
with friends you never got to know
and others who've been around
the neighborhood forever.

When I got to Samos, my bags, not filled with much really, were lost. I was totally unfazed. I had made it back, that was all that mattered.

You are gone
too far
for me
to ever see.
But you're
always here.
Heart beats.
Breath beats.

All of our bags
get lost
in the end
on the road
to our special
adventure.

They'll find our bags
if we're lucky
or if we're luckier
they're never found.
Then we're forced
to travel
lighter
freer.

I was back at Russ and Laura's white washed Samos home overlooking the Aegean.

It's best not to go barefoot.
Russ and Laura found
scorpions in the house.
Not lately though.
The cats take care of them.

The silhouettes of the King and Queen mountains across the water still slumbered serenely. The Fat Guy's Café became even more central, a spot to sit alone with my friends.

At sunset on the terrace there's the Aegean.
The cicadas, the morning glories slowly close,
the sleepy King and Queen mountaintops have not awakened yet
across the shimmering steel blue water.
And it's best they rest for months or millennia,
residing in their paradise of eternal love.
Let them inspire men and women able to see them,
mirror their constancy, ecstasy, serenity, loyalty, silent song.

This morning in the Fat Guy's Café.
The two chubby sons run the place now,
pirouette, dance and delicately serve tourists but mostly locals.
"White caps are the friends of men,"
Russ said as we walked down the steep rutted lane from home.
"Where's that from?" I asked.
"Me! Can't I say things like that too?"

Back in paradise, on Samos again, I re-examined the gardens— quietly in the morning and early evenings. I touched each tree, the stone walls, the wells, reacquainted myself with my old friends who had helped to make me whole four years before.

The walnut tree has grown three feet wider
since I last stood beneath its wide floppy leaves.
I'm too late for the pears this year.
The grass is sticky with rotten fruit and tiny flies
(Russ claims bore tiny holes into the pears
and also into our skin if given the chance.)
The wild figs are as big as cherries.
The pomegranates swing in sea breezes,
green and glad, maturing crimson.
Last night on my back I listened to the sea,
calm in the small blue room,

star-filled, wondering, grateful.
At peace
with loss
which isn't loss at all
which isn't about
loss
which is
Just how it is
as you once said softly.
Not sadly anymore,
calmer, with acceptance
openness, completion,
breathing, seeing, tasting
moving on along the road.
Baby I'm ready to go for a walk
if you are.

I spent more time with Russ on the second trip; it was harder for Russ to get around so we sat together, talked a lot, listened, read, watched, and shared the silence.

Considering his medical options
Russ, a fiery 86, grumbled,
"My legs are revolting against me."
And he conceded he needs to moderate his alcoholic intake.
Surveying his Samian universe in town at the square
under his white cotton hat and huge dark shades
the aging lion roared:
"I don't drink the hard stuff like before . . .
I just cut back—but a beer at lunch is alright.
Anything but abstention!
You have to live
or else you dry up."

Each summer once the house was open, the wild cats returned, often with kittens.

The mid-morning sun
burns and cleanses
the overturned plastic blue pail
spotted with concrete.
Morning glories stretch yearning for the sea.
Three tan male cats crunch their pebbly food
then one by one silently climb cement steps,
and lean deep into a yellow pail of water
to wash down breakfast.

The first trip to the Scopos Taverna felt very different on my second trip
to Samos, four years later. When we entered and found a table, I looked for
Karen and Yannis but didn't spot them. The place seemed more touristy but
somehow strangely still, vacant; there weren't as many tables and chairs out.
Where were the smells of roasting fish and meat, and the irresistible cooked
food laid out for guests?

Cicadas.
Is that Irish step dancing music?
The kid brought me small fried fish and eggplant salad.
Angelic music now, a bit spacey, fit for mourning I thought,
in Scopos Cafe at Mykali Beach.
Laura explained there's an outdoor movie theater in the mountains
where you sit at tables and have pizza and wine.
"It's my favorite movie theater in the world."
Russ sniffs with outrage, rustles the paper filled with "catastrophes and lies"
"Va-fun-gool!" he thunders from a height I haven't reached yet.
Greek outlaw, desperado, philosopher, artist,
despite his protestations
American son of Thoreau and Tom Paine.

Mykali flows deep and gray and blue
profound like your eyes used to be.
I wish I could write how my heart swells like the sea,
ebbs like love songs sung by wine-drunk doves and cheerful dolphins.
Karen isn't here in the cafe this year— she's at home down the road.
Two energetic young guys in baggy shorts

deposit five-foot speakers and an electric piano for performances on weekend nights.
"Like dreams do" a pop song croons.
A skinny guy in a black t-shirt with "Red Lion" on the back
serves us and his earring glitters.
His pale skin and dark sunken eyes explain
it's been party time for a very long time.
And so the Scopos Café at Mykali Beach rocks on dear.
But planetary, monumental Yannis Scopos died of liver cancer
in April or May, not sure.
"It was fast" from what Laura said.
Not much left of my wine
but with the last drop I toast gigantic Yannis
and his poor lost, hiding Australian Karen
who now has to fend for herself with her Greek in-laws
on Samos and beyond,
all of sudden
out of the blue.
Seas, the dry hills, the deserted olive groves,
eastern sexy, techno music pounds.
The beat goes on,
no matter what we do or say.

We all come
to the edge of land
naked and searching
to find the secret
on the surface
of the glittering
mysterious sea.

A pipe burst in the house. My bags were lost on the flight. The titanic muscular
Yannis was dead. Yet I felt serene, all was as it should be back in paradise. At the
beach no longer did I feel like I had landed from another planet. I belonged to
people again— my wound wasn't open and bleeding and paralyzing like before.

Pipes break unexpectedly.
We can't use the upstairs bathroom for the weekend.

My bags were lost on the flight.
In the tiny bathroom Laura painted with the girl in the tub
the hot and cold water faucets are reversed.
A couple of cab drivers were hyper and aggressive.
For some reason the water tanks aren't full.
And Yannis Scopos is dead.
Yet the sea still sparkles and cradles determined swimmers.
Cicadas sing cool jazz.
Middle-aged women go topless beside their proud husbands
who overflow their miniature thong swimsuits.
Splashing kids shout and young studs sweat and preen coolly.
Under cedar and waving bamboo,
facing the laughing mountains
I take a volcanic joyous piss.

Listening to Jobim sung live, a memory arrived. The Brazilian cabbie I hailed back in New York on Christmas Eve during that life I can never have back said something that proved true. Listening to Gal Costa sing the immortal Jobim live does change your life, makes you more alive, jogs you back to living, to wanting to love again, over and over, to want to be in love with love once more.

Christmas Eve morning
and you are dying my love.
Frantic, rushing, burning
I jumped into a cab
uptown to buy high-end takeout
from a chic Italian place on First and 79th Street
for one of the three Christmas dinners I planned that sad final season
as I tried to celebrate the holidays
though I knew I was losing you forever.
Hauling five plastic bags of delicacies for you and the kids
into the taxi the cabbie answered he was from Brazil.
For a moment I was jolted from our whirlwind spiral
and I breathed deeply and smiled back
and I asked, "What about Jobim?"
I quietly asked about Tom Jobim.

"You must listen to Gal Costa sing Jobim live," he said.
I saw his eyes flash in the rearview mirror,
his arms pump up and down, his head bounce with laughter.
"This changes your life.
Gal Costa sings Jobim live.
You must have it!
This changes your life."
I listen to Gal Costa this moment at Mykali Beach on my iPod.
Beautiful women and men in sun glasses
run to catch the blue Aegean
through the straits between two worlds
which I cross
in time to the effortless swinging hips
of the sexy world of Jobim.

I'm deeply moved
when a woman runs her hands
unconsciously through her hair,
tips her heads back,
caresses and straightens their hair,
slowly opens and closes her eyes
facing the light
like the sun and moon
making love in infinite space.

Though I brought my iPod, I didn't crave music plugged into my head on the
second trip. The natural sounds around me, or silence, was usually enough to
fill and inspire me.

Quiet is my music.
Silence soothes me best
on my journey into summer.
I don't need songs of love or lamentation.
I carry them within like breath, like sight.
The laughter of those small girls there,
refined cat paw steps at sunrise on the cement veranda,
buzzing circling bees, the shooshing sea wind in the cypresses and firs,

droning air conditioners, Greek café conversation half-audible,
the mysterious intonations of the seductive sea.
Voices lost are ever-present
miraculously orchestrated in mundane
hearty forkfuls of moment-by-moment electric now.
The two cypresses sway
to gentle Sunday morning breezes.
Under the pomegranate tree ants
climb the shiny green garden hose.
The gray blue water runs to the bay.
The chained dog on the terrace below
races back and forth whimpering.
Olive trees shiver in the chill.
Lemons calmly bob on branches.
Floppy palms wave at the sun.
Laura paints in her small studio.
Russ rests and reads.
Hushed beginning of another day.
Only the raven on the pole speaks
and I think I know what he's saying.

Russ bursts with oracular declarations and musings. He wanted to entertain
me; and self-conscious showman that he is, I believe he thinks I will write down
most of what he says—he was right, of course.

"All you have to do
is wake up
and see the world is filled with miracles,
the sea, the rocks, the sun, this glass,"
Russ said in a new café on the north side of the island
as Laura serenaded him with "You Don't Own Me" and "Leader of the Pack."
"Why did you come to Samos?"
Laura asked softly this morning as she descended the blonde
wooden handmade lighthouse staircase from her studio.
"Why did you come here the first time right after Gail died?"
Earlier Russ said quietly by the kitchen table,
"I read part of your poems last night— it's sad and beautiful."

"Everything you wrote brought back memories," Laura said sweetly.
On my walk to town for the Sunday Greek paper for Laura
I had half an ice coffee at the Fat Guy's Café.
(The proper name of the café is Hera Café I learned today.)
I guess I came to Samos because I'm connected to the Mediterranean
and with Russ and Laura I am close enough to be family
but far enough way to be really free.
"We know each other for over 30 years— before the kids were born,"
I answered Russ, whose white wild man cotton hat was pulled tight down on his head.
Barricaded behind his shades, he propped his arms like an ancient king on the table
which was covered with a shiny white table cloth with the map of Samos in blue.
The roasted goat, not my favorite, was passable, the dolmades inedible.
I devoured the chopped meat kabobs in tomato sauce with fries.
Russ sipped his mid-day iced Heineken in a frozen mug.
Since the house lemonade turned out to be canned Fanta I drank white wine.
I came for safety I suppose, to be protected yet set on fire in a timeless world
of killing cleansing sun and cool glittering starry nights.
Because I can watch the sea for hours unmolested,
hear the surf thunder syncopated with cicadas
and Greek pop music beat in time with my heart.

I sat for hours late one afternoon at the small beach near the house.

Ruined hotel like a classical memory.
Techno Greek pop and cicadas.
I pile stones on my towel
so it won't fly away.
A voluptuous woman in her 50s
in a wide red straw hat
lifts the brim
kisses her close-cropped gray-haired man
by the sea at sunset on Samos.

Each
face
the surface
of swirling
worlds.

Stopping at a grotto during Russ' morning "constitutional"
we marveled at wiry gray trees
growing deep into layers of brown rock.
Those are tough trees
to grow like that.

I took a long walk out towards Nisi Beach, miles from the house. It was dry
and sunny, deceptively so. I didn't have the sense to remember to bring water.
I was alone on the road beside the brilliant sea. I kept thinking how lucky I
was, how lucky I have been, despite the losses and heartaches. This is the basis
of gratitude, I suppose.

I marched along thinking about the Greek work for luck, *tikhli*. And it became
a kind of walking mantra as I strode solo under the most fabulous blue sky
you can imagine and beside a supercharged brilliantly blue-green crashing sea.
Getting thirsty, not sure how much more I had to go, I turned around after
almost two hours, walked back to small, scalloped Gagou Beach, close to the
house.

Magenta flowers overflow stubborn tan walls
trying to reach the restless sea.
Small cars peel by inches away.
Motorbikes with kids in bathing suits
zoom past laughing on their way to Nisi Beach.
Each dusty hairpin turn planted with memorials
to drivers whose luck held out.
Laura said the Greek word for luck is *tikhli*
These squat stone memorials chant
Tikhli behind sooty glass windows.
Tikhli where a candle flickers beside a photo of a young soldier
from an unnamed war savagely fought in paradise.
Ttikhli memorials that look just like condo developments.
Tikhli painted square cement block barbecues,
colored blue with miniature white domes and crosses.
Tikhli hovers with the flies buzzing over immaculate garbage bins in the sun.
Abandoned stone mansions brood
behind rusted iron gates and steep stone entrances choked with brush.

Tikhli freshly painted in blues and reds on hotels perched on sheer rock face.
Tikhli floats above the small gray islands in the blinding, blue, white-capped sea.
And on the trip back home down along the narrow
winding lane to cozy Gagou Beach and the Vergina Café
I stop beside a small cat purring in the shade.
Tikhli, tikhli.
The white cat watches me intently
under bougainvillea, wild fig and hibiscus.
A small white cat watches me.
Tikhli, tikhli.
I hear the sea whoosh through bamboo and palm.
Tikhli, the cat murmurs to me.
Tikhli, I answer.
Tikhli, it will be.

At the Vergine Café at small, scallop-shaped Gagou Beach I wrote and drew in
the black book a friend had given me as a gift for the trip.

Chicken souvlaki and fries.
A busty unnaturally vertical blond German woman
in a see-through wrap-around strides from the beach,
tows kids with pink plastic pails and luminescent green shovels.
Skinny unshaven Greek guys frown and strut
in tight cut-off tees, skin tight jeans and oversize dark shades.
My white wine is frosty and sweet and smiles.
My blue-eyed quiet waiter was right.
All of it tastes good.

A majestic tan Greek woman
with a magenta head scarf
and flowery bikini
waits for her daughter in the taverna
sitting on the edge of a stone wall.
She stares through the trees
to the sea with faraway eyes,
braids her thick dark hair,
then stands with her hands on her hips,

erect like a classic marble sculpture
and shouts to her son invisible in the bathroom:
"Hey let's go!
Come on! Let's go!
We don't have all day!"

After my meal, I walked up the hillside that overlooks Gagou Beach and for
hours, with my Yankee cap on and slathered with sunscreen, I became one
with what I saw— united.

Love is how
the rocky cove
embraces
the late day sea,
for another day,
so we can float,
splash, laugh,
ascend once more.

Breathing,
taking
a chance
on life,
love,
again.

Breakfast was a major social event. Russ had usually been awake for hours—he
rarely slept more than a couple of hours. Like an impatient, human alarm
clock, he began to whistle—very loud—when he thought Laura and I should
get up and emerge to have coffee, which he had prepared for us, with feta
cheese and honey on bread.

This morning at breakfast— buttered toast and coffee—
before coughing and denouncing "disaster capitalism,"
Russ said that the Greek poet Sikilenos and a friend
intoxicated by the sheer power of their words and visions
apparently thought they could literally raise the dead.

So the pair tried one night to actually pull off this miracle.
But after many futile, frustrating minutes trying to bring life back to a dead man,
the poet's friend utterly exasperated at the corpse's lack of enthusiasm for their plan,
stared at Sikelianos, and outraged, he finally sputtered,
Such stubbornness! Such stubbornness!

Late morning, still sitting by the kitchen table, while Laura worked in her
studio, Russ recalled a dead friend, explained how he was still around, always
present.

I see my old friend Daphnes
out there in the stone wall.
He's right there— I see him.
Wow— behind the walnut tree!
And out that window— that tree looks just like Genghis Khan.
It's fantastic— right there on the olive tree.
Genghis Khan has come back!
You see his eyes and his nose?
Look! Look!
How can we not see that people are never gone,
their memorials are the rocks and stones and trees.
They live right here with us.
They can been seen all the time.

Russ constantly assessed his life, his relative lack of recognition despite a great
body of world class work, his life of restlessness and rebellion of never settling
in one place long enough to set down roots and curry favor with critics and
gallery owners, his disgust with the commercial world of art. Despite having
studied with Leger, Siqueiros, having lived in Paris with Beauford Delaney (in
Paris, he threw a party for James Baldwin when he published his first book),
hanging out at the Cedar Bar in its heyday, hundreds of the master paintings
are in storage in New York, a place Russ ironically calls "the morgue."

Russ has worried his life like dog with a bone, turned it over and over though
I saw that he seemed free of the vying and scheming for commercial success,
fighting for renown. There was the life and there was the work, and that was
it, what it amounts to in the end. His fierce independence though belied a hurt

that still rankled him. He knew he had delivered "the goods," and he knew his
constant state of lucid, romantic rebellion had worked against him.

Sometimes I think I see too much.
You reach a certain age
and you don't give a damn
about the newspapers,
what people say.
If I don't know myself by now
where am I?
You have to say, Fuck them all!
You can't be too quiet in this life.
You have to go your own way,
live your own life.
Who gives a shit what they think.
If you don't know who you are
by this age where are you?

They had a chance
to make it all
paradise.
Instead they created
hell.

We spent more time in the Fat Guy's Café.

White-haired men sit in cafes, smoke, talk.
The ferry waits to leave Samos Town.
Costas and Georgas, the two sons,
run the Fat Guy's Café now.
Their parents with their grand children
scamper through the café, their great life school.
Both overweight brothers still move gently and lightly,
radiate energetic angelic sweetness.
Yesterday it was over 100 and muggy,
Samos Day with huge crowds at a festival in Pythagorio.
A family dressed like American Indians pack

and leave the small Samos Town square where they performed.
They live in Athens, Costas explains.
"They are poor people— they live on handouts."
These ersatz Native American buskers
look like they're from South America,
wander like gypsies
island to island during summers
when tourists and Euros are plentiful.
Tonight we're seeing two pop singers at an outdoor concert.
Stars in Greece— Dimitra Galanie and Elefteria Arvaniftaikie
in a school yard behind the Samos Museum.
If we're lucky, they'll be a moon.

I made another day trip to Turkey, a pilgrimage to Ephesus. This time funding the tour bus from the dock in Turkey was ridiculously easy— you literally walked right into it once you left the boat. How had I missed it the last time? Blocked, blinded by death, I believe, distracted by lost love.

Our Turkish tour guide on the bus was a pretty super star—and she knew it.

Sexy, vain, petite.
The dark round tour guide
to Ephesus coos,
"Our country Turkey
is a Muslim country.
But we are not fanatics.
I have to tell people this.
You see.
You see the city.
You see *me*.
You see *me*."

I wrote a series of haiku about the day trip in Turkey.

Ruined lost Ephesus
now means broiling tourists live.
Marble killing spa.

The stone library
with three thousand precious scrolls.
How much did they learn?

The angry sea fled.
then the great city withered,
expired slowly.

Cities simply die—
from war, earthquakes, diseases,
incrementally.

Italian tourists
cluster, laugh and speak loudly.
The ruins laugh too.

If you rated, you
built great marble monuments
to your own glory.

"After a while it's
all just rock," he said, blue eyes
glittering, smiling.

He's smart enough to
take your order, your money,
buy houses, land, girls.

This fine silk carpet.
took two girls two years to weave.
A Turkish Rolls Royce.

Grand Harbor Road leads
nowhere now— to brush, parched land.
Once the sea splashed here.

Deserted city
with no songs, cries, no lovers,
no trading in life.

By the huge camel:
If you want to take pictures
You must pay money.

Thinking of a city
with no inhabitants left—
great ruined Ephesus.

Dark illegal men,
broken, huddled deportees
on my morning walk.

Our hip, confused guide
"Please go waste time in the shops."
Her smile incandescent.

So easy to find
the Meander Tour buses.
Not lost, but found now.

On the ferry back, I felt the pain cutting me apart again.

Dying
for your
arms.
Dying
in your
arms.
Dying
in my
arms.
Dying
for your
arms.

Mornings I took walks, most times alone, with Russ when he felt strong enough
for a short stroll. We have to move on, no matter what, we have to move on.

Ancient trees
uprooted
slowly by time
swiftly in storms,
or cut by the unsettled hands of men,
leave deep wounds
in the rocky brown earth
that are gradually filled
by winter rains,
summer sun,
winds,
other growing things.

Composed, at peace, one morning I meditated about my life and profound connection to my children, Danny and Emily, my two wings. How they had weathered the initial part of the storm of the loss of their mother, and how as with me, our grief as a family would take on unpredictable shapes and sounds and forms. I prayed that it would bring the three us only closer, as Gail wanted and wrote to each of us before she had to leave.

How the sun burns truths into stubborn rock faces,
The craggy shore gracefully calms the churning sea.
Clouds cast cool shadows that race across the mountains and groves.
The sea lifts men and women to distant places.
Birds find their nests at sunset and sing.
The wind caresses so many trees in darkness.
Excited stars welcome the lazy tired returning moon.
Prayers for my children this morning.

Russ talked about his father a great deal, a vigorous man who had lived to almost 100. An authoritarian, old school patriarch, Russ' father was extremely jealous of his wife, Russ' mother. Russ painted a fabulous portrait of "the old man", and I saw that Russ had turned into a version of the portrait, whether he knew it or not.

My father had a beautiful voice.
He could have been a professional singer.
I mean he could control his voice.
Back then everybody sang
or played an instrument.
You had to entertain yourself.
Not like today.
It came from inside.
There was no TV, no radio, no Internet.
Now everything comes from the outside.
Back then there were feast days and the music in the church,
what was going on in the café, in the taverna.
My father would gather the musicians.
One was a black gypsy who played the violin.
It all came from inside, you understand?
You had to find ways to entertain yourself,
make music, art, you had to do it yourself.
Now it all comes from the outside.
So the inside is dormant, uncultivated.
Not like before.

I was surprised to learn that the kitchen table, the omphalos of the Samos house, where simply everything that mattered happened and was discussed and investigated and sung, was actually from North Carolina where Russ lived with his first wife, the mother of his three daughters. In the 70s, Russ and his wife ran a summer art school on Samos and Laura and her sister were students. Laura stayed—just never left.

When I sit at the table
I rescued from the North Carolina dump
the faces in the stone wall in the garden
recognize me and wave.
The eyes in the olive tree out that window there
squint from the sun this time of day.
The mouth in the stone steps
I built by hand with heavy stones
invites me to take a long walk,
to dance again.

Lying in the pale blue room, I thought of her.

I remember her shy smile,
the back of her soft tapering neck,
the way her hair fell upon her shoulders,
the curve of her hips, her lower back, her lips,
hands and feet I knew like my own.
Her eyes flashed with deep blue gray passion,
widened like a child's,
grew serious when she looked up
from a book, from fixing dinner.
I remember her immense silences too.
Her purple, misty, unknowable silences,
sunset-like, sweet, mysterious,
serene, challenging like the sea's face,
her eyes deep wells of being and feeling,
telling me everything I needed to know
with no fanfare,
simply,
hand in hand.

Walking to town for groceries, Laura and I passed an extraordinary mansion
and I remarked upon its size and color. Then Laura told me the story of the
old women we just happened to pass on the road going into town that day. It
turned out the old woman who had said a few friendly words to Laura in Greek
as she walked in the opposite direction was part of the story of the grand
house that I had admired. Laura explained that when she first came to Samos
each summer she used to rent a room from the old woman, named Irene.

Irene was a dirt poor girl
from a mountain village on Samos.
She cleaned for an old man in town.
She eventually married him
for his mansion but she took good care of him.
He died, she married a man more her age.
He worked in a small shop Irene opened

on the ground floor of the pale green mansion.
Then husband #2 died.
Back luck, I guess.
I passed Irene on the road into town this morning.
She's in her late 70s now, still a sweet woman.
But she was young when I rented her house 30 years ago.
And anyway she took care of the old man.
Who else would?
So why shouldn't she have a big house?
She wouldn't have had anything otherwise.
Just a girl from a village
with nothing, nobody, Irene.

Russ said that when he was a boy he pushed his grandmother down a hill because she had been mean to him; it was poignant and funny how the injustice of the memory still angered him. Russ still felt this was a brave, boyhood act of liberation, a successful fight again oppression. In my mind his story merged into ancient history, interpreted by a contemporary scholar.

What we know of the Great General
from a partially preserved ancient scroll found in a villa in Heraon:
" . . . *in his father's village in the north* . . .
The old woman dug the branches with thorns
deep into his arm as punishment . . .
Though only 10 years old at this time
The boy . . . *not large* [*"forceful"* or *"tall"?*]
pushed her away . . .
as she fell down the slope
he cried out: Do not ever
do that to me again! . . ."
Later with his legions fighting heroically for the empire,
the General amused his commanders one night by the fire
saying, "It wasn't so bad . . .
My grandmother didn't roll *that far* . . ."

A hymn to the sun, which saved me.

Please
sun.
Burn
away
my
self
so I can
love
again.
Free.

Early on a Saturday night, the three of us sat at the kitchen table before
dinner in order to listen on the ancient boom box to a weekly local Greek
radio program that played American pop classics. Laura sang along as she
quietly finished a crossword puzzle. Russ, not very enthusiastic about the
bottom feeder pop music bouncing around the kitchen, was for the most part
quiet, though from time to him, he grumbled, shifted in his seat, rustled his
newspaper, and seemed ready to burst.

Write down the sunrise,
how sun flees too.
Be brave enough,
as the weekly Greek radio show
with American pop classics
coughs and rattles from the dusty boom box.
Laura finishes another crossword puzzle
on the kitchen table rescued from the North Carolina dump.
"Sister Morphine," the Righteous Brothers, Marianne Faithful, the Monkeys.
"They usually do better than this,"
Laura says softly her head down as she works.
The sun's orange and Russ nibbles chocolate
to kill the taste of his medicine named Tres Bon.
"Greece was different back then," she says wistfully,
inspired by the half-hour of radio music, remembering the vibrant 70s,
when Russ had his famous summer art school on the island,
when the junta tried to throw him in prison for being a free man,
and hippies, wannabe artists, youngsters away from home for the first time,

lost souls, Laura herself, landed on Samos to make paintings, listen to music,
dance where the ancients came to pray.

"Leonard Cohen lived for seven years on Hydra,"
Laura explains in response to my question about why I see the Canadian poet's face
in the papers nearly every day along with forest fires and scandals.

Back then it seemed simpler, she explained— painting, songs, hanging out in
tavernas, drugs, crying, dramatic scenes, sex, the Love Generation on the loose.

After summer adventures on Samos, a young actress returned home
to become a cultural minister, an Italian poet and artist finally couldn't go on,
ended his life in the cold with secrets and delirious pain.

"Crimson and Clover" in the kitchen merges with the wind, the waves.

Crimson and clover,
Over and over.
Crimson and clover,
Over and over . . .

And then Russ suddenly erupts, begins to recite the final pages of
The Odyssey by Kazantzakis by heart in Greek,
and then he launches into the beginning of *The Divine Comedy*
in swirling Italian with defiance and eternal certainty,
and then we all stop as the music on the radio ends,
and we just look for a long time at each other,
in silence, moments at day's ending,
but it is really the now, the moment stilled,
perfected, essential,
and forever.
We just look
and we understand,
we know.

Crimson and clover
Over and over.
Crimson and clover
Over and over . . .

Looking back and forward, standing in the garden a few days before the end of
my second trip, I imagined the essence of a past life, filled with joy, feasting,
with laughter and dance, a life that can never return, doesn't need to.

We danced in the heat
on the stone veranda.
We said summer would never end.
It didn't rain till October.
We sang The Wanderer,
Curtis Mayfield, Pavarotti,
Springsteen, the Beatles, Stevie Wonder.
The wine from town
didn't taste bad in my sangria concoction.
We ate on blankets on the wild oregano
under the walnut which was a sapling then.
We twirled our hysterical kids and our friends' children too
in time to the music and the sound of the sea.
My love, we said if there was paradise
this was it— it couldn't get any better
than this.
Amazing how easy
to write these words to you
dancing alone with my iPod
still this crazy fervor
facing the turbulent, knowing sea.

Serene remembrance, another tribute, to her.

Now drink the gentle breeze
at sunset.
There's half a moon again.
Last night during dinner
Laura laughed and said:
Look, half the moon's on vacation— it's August!
I sit and admire the moon's revealed right side.
The neighbor calls his small scruffy dog
who wanders invisible in the grape vines.
Hectora! Hectora!
Water runs from a spout somewhere.
Sea winds move the pines and cypresses.
A bird coos.

I hear cars pass in the dark.
A plump fly buzzes on the low blue wooden table
Russ built and Laura painted
with a wreath of olive leaves, pomegranates,
two doves kissing, a border of classic Greek waves.
Cicadas, barking dogs.
I breathe
a ticker tape parade of you.

I am going
where glistening waves flow
in honest afternoon heat,
confident, joyous,
laughing, boisterous,
not caring
rolling home

As my second journey ended and days quieted and closed in succession, each one
singular and unique and never to be repeated, the world became transfigured,
elevated, concentrated and deeply felt. I was okay, shaky at times, but I had
made it. I was back, within the world, inhabiting my own life.

I was grateful for the simple chance each day to get it right. And life embraced
me again, uplifted me, and I prayed without words, just by breathing, being, to
be worthy of its eternal power, to continue to open to men and women, to never
to stop watching the sea, clouds, faces, the sky at night with its numberless
stars, stars so distant and yet so hopeful, beacons of love and life, stars full of
so many fresh mornings.

The evening cicadas serenade.
I sit on the empty stone veranda.
Sunset, the sleeping cats.
The aluminum ladder lies on its side
beside the abandoned white stained canvas picnic umbrella.
Rising half-moon.
Pomegranates dangle just above my head.
The slate gray sea shivers.

Dancing palms, the two great cypresses
raise me, fill me, lead me,
remind me
it's all about imagination.
Silhouettes of two silent doves
sit on top of the electric pole.
Stars will appear soon.

When I Was in New York

How People Die

People don't die
like they die in the movies.
They just get pale.
There's no music
except in your head maybe.
They thrash, twitch,
moan, wheeze,
struggle to breathe,
try to get comfortable.
They speak in garbled ways
you never heard before,
words you almost understand.
And then they grow quiet.
Then there's nothing
behind their eyes.
It just happens
like that
just how it is
in space
at that moment.
People die that way.

Join the Party/email to WK

My birthday dinner is off for good now.
Malle is on the TV screen after take out— his Indian documentary.
So many dark bodies, faces, arms, toes, eyes.
We are in another place.
Faces of beggars, huge, moving, seas of brown faces,
then one, this one, this one now, I want to share with you.
This face,—close up—brown shining eyes, wrapped in rags, scraggly mustache,
just his dark, gaunt, haunting face, rotted teeth.
This dialogue now, as I type:
-Why are you here?
-They picked me up on the street. I haven't eaten anything for several days.
Calcutta is a difficult city.
-Are you from Calcutta?
-No, I come from far away.
When I was 20 I left my family,
since then I have been traveling here and there on foot.
I visit holy places. I'm a hermit. I beg for my food.
-Why did you give up everything at age 20?
-Because life is an illusion.
Yeah, maybe it's the Twilight Zone.
Maybe life's a canceled TV classic
we dimly remember and conjure half-wrong.
But what's the difference anyway,
it's only memory and memory's like that, not real,
you know what I mean,
the illusion of remembering.
The Twilight Zone is always just beyond what we understand,
Like life the illusion,

what we can accept, what we know, or want to know,
Life moves forward only,
a step ahead of us always,
just beyond our reach, knowing.
I sit here on the couch with furry Giuletta, who had kittens once,
starved on the street, was mistreated, remains skittish,
beautiful—a diva devoted just to me.
Some girlfriends don't like my cat friend.
(One didn't even take to the fabulous beloved feline Fellini either
and every human who encountered that wise departed soul, loved him).
Giuletta sheds, messes up stuff, make some swell up, tear, cough.
Causing blindness and suffocation's ample reason to dislike her, I suppose.
Really though she represents my own messy, untidy life.
Demanding, needy, proud, aloof, wayward, unpredictable, confused,
unable to say what I mean.
Eating out of cans after work, drinking wine, listening to music all hours.
Lost and visionary, I cling to basics— food, shelter, a clean litter box,
a little soothing now and then,
someone to gently scratch my back.
Funny life, no?
From Malle to Calcutta, from the Twilight Zone to cat hairs,
the improbable dance of competing needs and wants and dreams and loves.
Join the party, you write.
For sure.
Encore/Xxxx G

When I Was in New York

here

      not here

not here

      here

when

     I

        was

           in New York

This Poem

how lonely
on this plane
knowing
I can't
ever
share
this poem
with you
my love

White Owl

Across the wood paneled meeting room
I see the two Audubon white owls
vivid, still
perched on a leafless tree.
The pair remind me
of your special dream friend,
the white owl who advised
you during meditation.
When you suffered
you and your owl always met
in the same meadow in the dreamy woods
and the bird rubbed your check with its snowy wings.
You wept as you recounted
the kindness of your magic white owl
wise enough inside you to be gentle
compassionate enough to soothe you,
to love you for yourself alone forever.

Hair

My hair, you wrote in red pen
on the white sealed business envelope
I found in your desk drawer yesterday.
How could you know, my fabulous lost love
that I also wrote, wiping tears from my face,
Gail's hair on a white sealed envelope that I also hid.
I see that till the end we both protected each other
from what life is capable of doing to us.
We both knew when
you had to cut your sensual, thick brown hair
something momentous had occurred,
a threshold was crossed.
Like two characters in a fairy tale
marching resolute hand-in-hand in the Dark Wood
we passed a fork in the Open Road
that foretold our parting was not far off.
We both just knew, suffered silently,
tried to cheer each other, with smiles, poems, caresses
and hugs in a world growing
so much more alone cold.

If

If you
were here
now
I would hug
you
tight.
Kiss you
deep
as cicadas sing
in summer
just for us.

Walks

A walk
down
the block
is an odyssey
too.

Death
is just
stepping
from this
room
to the next.

Rainbows

"Who takes care of you?"
she said her husky red voice
on fire in bed.
And then we walked and talked,
laughed and wondered
beneath three rainbows.
Open the door baby,
and just keep going.

Small Trees

The bottoms of small brown trees
are bundled in burlap
in ordered rows
the cold night before they're born
where short blonde wooden stakes
wait pounded into the dark soil.
My shadow caresses each
as I walk home wondering
which will get to hear
the ice cream truck on July 4th
and which won't make it till fall.

Pigeon

What was left of the pigeon
the neat, compact gray pile
crushed by tires, barely missed by rushing feet,
disintegrating inevitably, quietly
into the blackness of the street bed,
feathers compressed, but a few strays
fluttering for some reason
on the crosswalk near the southeast corner
of West 95th Street and Broadway.
Hot and tired end of a summer work day
I sat on a park bench on the mall
and suddenly understood:
This is it—this is the beauty of beauty itself.
This is what's left
for us
distilled
to dream upon
what's left for us to imagine,
the exhilaration of soaring
darting through trees,
swooping suddenly down past chess games in parks,
children and balloons, napping babysitters,
lovers on soft newly cut grass,
all of us lost and out on a day pass,
this memory of birdsong at dusk,
this chorus in New York unheard,
this strutting under legs
hoping for crumbs.

Awakening

I want
to awaken
to a child's smile
with eyes of wonder
to a new day.

Shadows

every thing has a shadow
every thing
even high noon
even night itself, even darkness
every thing has a shadow
alone
with others
every thing has a shadow
the wind, the sun,
rain, mountains, kisses, babies, corpses
dreams, promises, hopes,
every thing has a shadow
every thing has a shadow
every thing has a shadow
trees, the cat beside me,
Nina Simone singing
Who Knows Where the Time Goes
has a shadow too
every thing has a shadow
every thing
even you
even me
even these words
every syllable
each sound
has a shadow
every sound
has a shadow
like the sound
of love itself
has a shadow
like—I love you

I/You/2

I feel
happier
with you
in the world.

I want
you
to be
happy.

Trees

nobody talks
to trees
says thank you
for shade
touches them
hugs them
as they rise
with faith
in autumn
in New York

Renaissance Love

Life soaks me Renaissance orange
and her thick dark hair flows with the curtains
in the breeze at night in the Village
on that special iron bed from Italy
after we made love again.
If we are measured at all
it is by how we've loved,
how we've been ravished and cherished,
elevated and blessed,
discarded like trash,
how we've dreamed love songs
in parking lots, embraced wet in the rain
on bridges in storms, panted intertwined on park benches.
We swam together that night,
her body elastic long and undeniable.
You're strong, she whispered.
And then we slept,
floated, gently, completely.

Gary Zarr

Gone

I'm just going
to rest
for 10 minutes.
And then she never
came back.

Beach Night

"The conversation was so pretentious,
but I loved eavesdropping,"
she said by sea, the blackness
sheltered strangers on the edge
of where you can go.
"Hey look, I think those people are naked!"
Distant laughter, a small fire in the sand,
cascading, thundering waves.
She asked if I was comfortable
with her dancer's body resting on my chest,
between my legs
as we both faced the waves.
"What are you thinking?"
"Oh, not much."
Really though—
How lucky to be anonymous
under this canopy of searching stars,
holding someone like you so close,
so close, this close.
So close I feel your heart beat.

Gary Zarr

Small Tree

This cold spring night
I wonder who had taken
the time
to secretly plant
this baby evergreen
out in the center of the lawn
vulnerable
stranded in a sea of grass
where no tree
was ever meant to be.

The Sound

It is now
and so fast.
Don't you hear
the beating
of the wings?

Gary Zarr

Your Tree

I found the knobby gray tree
you touched
leaned on
to steady yourself
a moment, my love.
I held your arm
that early morning
as we slowly walked together
into another fresh spring.

Driving Too Fast

"My ride is here."
Springsteen sings Warren Zevon.
I can't see the ocean past the balcony blackness
further than the lights of South Beach.
Recorded crowds cheer, the dryer spins,
who cares about wine or forced laughter.
Let's vocalize with the universe for a while,
gargle starlight like candy store comic books.
These melancholy blue lights, the green ones, blink too.
It's so clear I'm in need of artificial inspiration.
Stops signs stare and I ignore them.
I'm driving too fast again through known dead zones.

To Bob

We fight to be free.
In a local Belgian place,
very tired tonight,
breathing, trying to.
Life is a door that opens
then slams closed in our faces without warning.
Society and the beating we take is a comic tragic attempt
to crush our spirit, domestic us.
Fuck it.
I believe in what you write, in what you feel and sigh and walk.
I believe in love everlasting.
I believe in passion, and in thought and dreaming,
and the touch, the smell, the taste.
Earth, spring, snow, rain, the sea, songs, laughter—from everywhere and all time.
I believe deeply and truly there is no end as there was never any beginning.
I believe in smiles, and children and animals.
I worship trees and clouds and mountains and rivers.
I believe in art, and poetry and writing, and physical exertion.
I believe in sex which equals the perpetual fornication with existence itself.
And I believe in the beauty and transcendence and inspiration of women,
of that special one right there, before us always.
I believe in this waitress who acts like she likes me but just wants a big tip.
And I believe in this place I sit this moment in time alone
and I know it is somehow eternally present.
I believe in those stars and the blackness between them
and everything that is, was and will be
and I believe in you totally and without condition, my friend.
I believe in me too when I am strong enough and rested enough,
and finally I believe in gratitude
which flows from me like spring flowers, like the wind,

like confessions to the sun,
like the kisses of life itself.
And I believe in nothing at all.
I believe in not believing
which is faith itself
smiling back in a mirror.

Two Trees

Two trees flower,
yearn for each other
at night.
The smell of wood
in the cool damp spring air.
Years they have patiently grown
across the path,
one day to finally fulfill
the promise
of touch.
Branches will dance
return to waiting branches.
Wet leaves laugh tenderly
within bouncing soft leaves.

Your Love

Always believe
you can sleep late
with your love
touching your side
the sheer curtain breathing
gently with the sea.
This familiar world of hair,
this neck, this back, these arms
I fall into again
where I belong.

The Dead

We have to let the dead go
to find their way into the sky
along invisible roads
we will travel one day.
We can wave to them,
even pat them on the back,
or tell them a joke or two,
because sometimes just kidding the dead
makes them feel so much better.

Dreamsville

Closer, easy.
Dreamsville.
This morning across the kitchen table
you smiled unconsciously, relaxed.
You smiled, quietly talked, laughed gently,
pulled your thick dark hair back,
tipped your sunflower face sideways,
gazed up deep brownishly somewhere,
and you smiled again.
You smiled
and for a moment I was reborn.

Poetry

Poetry is
where
we know
we should be
come back to
ourselves
where we belong
elevated
soaring
way out there
our feet firm
on the ground.

Home

We do
make it
home
over time
in waves
confused
bloody
with dreams
we've earned
certain
and golden.

Gary Zarr

Upstate at Night

we used to stare at nets of stars
the four of us enchanted
the moon blazed through black trees
the smell of fire wood
in the dark mountain valley
"Hey, I see the Big Dipper!"
"There's Orion— that's the hunter!"
we held hands and sang
in the cold night after eating too much
together as one
laughing in the dark
on those shooting star nights

The Line

It's just a line.
But it's the end of the world,
the horizon
outside my terrace in Miami.
This could be Hanoi, Paris, Rome, Rio, Istanbul, Bombay, Madrid.
Ancient eyes or eyes not yet born
would know that it's only just a line
that separates the sky from the sea.
But it's the end of the world
and I am the one who sees it now.

End

In the end darkness prevails
and the stars fly away
to where we cannot see them.
We float alone in a silent spot
within utter outer space
by ourselves,
gazing left and right,
up and down,
searching
for a faint flicker
a beating in time with the rhythm
of our own restless heart.

Nights

I gaze out
the bedroom window.
Moon in eclipse.
Where are you dear?

I softly say your name.
The moon vanishes.
It grows even darker.

Barefoot in the bedroom
I try to find the moon.
Apartment lights blink
across the deserted courtyard.

During the eclipse
cold winds blow fall trees.
Leaves soon no more.

Alone with the fleeing light
Get through this darkness.
A huge harvest moon's up next.

Stepping from the cab
the monumental hazy moon.
Rises over apartments, trees, me.

There's something
about the rain
slanting down
past street lights

on the other side
of the window
in the fall night

Before sunrise
branches of trees white,
muffled scraping of snow plows.
Thinking of you,
I weep.

Natural law—
The most beautiful
are not the hardiest.

A Dream

Last night in a dream
I saw myself as a painted portrait,
painstakingly drawn by me I think,
colorful in chalks and paint and pen.
Then the *me* out there moved,
came suddenly to life though still in a frame
or reflected in a mirror inches away.
The eyes began to roll, the head turn restlessly,
and then a fierce white light appeared
shining intense and pure, centered above my eyes.
Suspended in half-sleep, I grew too afraid
to stare at the profoundly powerful star
implanted like an eternal jewel in my mind.

Twins

The sun has an unseen twin
in deepest outer space
that we have not been able to find
whirling alone or with others in fun
beyond where humans lie.
Collapsed and dying, young and exploding,
or maybe a compact shadow sun
just ashes and elements and dreams,
a knowing kindred light,
a winking interstellar lover's eye
that teases and soothes
the molten core of our shattered heart.

Near Me

I wonder
what she really sees
her dark eyes open so wide
yet closed inside
as she leans with her cheek in her palm
her thin brown hair falls fanlike
early in the morning
in the local diner
at the next table.

The Fountain

The stone fountain gushed clear
in the lush garden wild with garlic and roses.
Small apples bobbed in bubbling green water
in the slanting orange late summer light.
We washed grapes from the tangled vine,
smelled spits of meat roasting on the fire.
The spearmint and wine mingled with
my father's laughter in the wind.
I hugged the world then,
and it hugged me back.

Museum

I'm not sure I can raise the money
to start the new museum I have in mind.
The only exhibitions offered to the public
will explore cultures we will one day obliterate
wage war against. Shows will examine the people,
how they speak, their stories and what they believe—
but only the people who hate us or soon will—
nations we will vow to annihilate in self-defense.
Posters promoting each exhibition
need only splash each country's name in bold bloody letters
and the public will kill each other to see the latest evil
in living color, live right before their eyes.
What better way to fulfill our educational mission
than to help the public fully understand
what they will be asked to destroy.

Notches

there's a sharp notch
cut deep into the silver
for each station
along the bracelet
of our journey

Heart

heart
so strong
grand
yet fragile
small
keeps beating
as light
comes on

Pillow

I try to recall
the final time
her soft round face
rested on the pillow
beside my grateful head.
I press my wet eyes
upon the holy spot
where her cheek was
desperate to find warmth
the lost fragrance of her.

A Girl's Memory

I love the smell of cut grass.
It reminds me of summers Upstate
in the country with my mother.
I always sat in my grandfather's huge chair.
It was sunny, my brother and I laughed.
We didn't have to do anything.
We just watched TV, went to the mall,
took walks in the woods behind the house,
ate lunch out on the old picnic table,
had ice cream cones on car trips.
At night I slept in my Mom's old room.
I liked it when my brother was there
because we knew the house had ghosts.
I loved to pet all the cats.
Once when my father came up for the week,
the four of us stood on the lawn after dinner
and we watched all the stars and we really laughed.

Expiration Dates

Mozart piano concerto #20, morning coffee at the card table.
The beach apartment is empty and that is full enough.
My brother spoke from snowy New York,
called to check in—seems the toilet needs fixing, the cat prospers.
-*Gary, you should check the expiration dates of things in your closets.*
-*Oh?*
-*Yeah. The mustard in the refrigerator, I think, is from two years ago.*
-*Oh. Ok.*
-*The lens cleaner in the closet. They are from three years ago.*
-*Ok.*
-*Yeah, you should check the expiration dates of things.*
He's right, of course.
We should pay attention to the expiration dates all around us.
We need to be wise consumers.
Finishing my granola, Mozart rises and falls
like distant gray blue waves beyond the palms.
Do we all come with our own expiration dates,
specific times that once we pass
we are totally on our own,
far from outstretched hands or a safe shoreline,
beyond which it is up to us
to stay or go, to live or die,
or to just die—over and over
and so live forever
reborn each time
like leaping dolphins
free finally and soaring at chilly dawn.

Seaweed

lines of dark seaweed
dry in the sun
washed up by waves
onto the scalloped sand
at night in the chill
under the huge yellow moon
when no one watches
when no one comes near the sea

Gary Zarr

Broken Wheel

The broken wheel
abandoned in the field
by the untended apple trees
surrounded by cans, overgrown weeds,
planks of wood, plastic bottles.
You can clearly see
where the tire tracks lead.

Lover

My soft cheek, my dark star
My question, my answer
My wonder, my flower
My darkness, my light
My drama, my stillness
My field, my river
My dancer, my actor
My hope, my fear
My moan, my shout
My song, my silence
My pain, my balm
My wonder, my anchor
My sun, my night
My dawn, my sunset
My dream, my dream
My answer, my question
My lover, my lover

Gary Zarr

Spring

Spring returns
for me
with flowers, sun,
friends like you.
The magic
is now.

Listening to Dylan in Great Barrington

Summer stars,
fireflies sing
sad rainy love songs
that reach my wanderer's lost blue heart.
The green arms of weeping trees
hang over two empty lawn chairs.
Consoling winds run through wet pines and ferns.
A cardinal called and flew towards me at breakfast.
I knew you were here
lost woman of the North Country.
One too many mornings . . .
and so much more.

The General's Dream

It was so long ago, lost in the orchards of his childhood.
His mother was always a dream to him.
Her face shone like the solitary smiling moon
making the dark world light again and clear.
She hugged and kissed him, soothed her precious little boy,
wiped his face and dried his eyes.
How they both would laugh
as she held him close
raised him to the cloudless sky while the leafy fig trees sang.
Having conquered the known world,
the general always dreamed of his mother
the night before combat.
He had grown so used to slaughter,
dismembered children no longer moved him,
nor their bloated bluish, putrid parents,
lifeless arms beseeching the sun
to save their doomed sons and daughters.
Though the general could not remember her voice
his mother always came in a dream the night before battle.
His mother always came when he was in need.
And so invincible, fierce, armed and lethal,
he fought enfolded in her protective, golden, maternal embrace.

Waitress

When she was an old woman,
she remembered one night ages ago in Miami,
when she worked as a waitress,
her dark brown hair and her eyes wild,
when she stayed out all night.
A smiling man in an orange shirt
asked her name
when she came with his food.
Elizabeta, Elizabeta,
she heard her voice
under the moon.
She understood that moment
that she would always remember
this man and his sad eyes and crooked smile
and how he carefully wrote down *Elizabeta*
in a small notebook as she walked away
so hot and sexy and young back then.

Gary Zarr

Lucky Wind

Imagine the joy of this galloping afternoon sea wind
as it whips the tops of palms
tickles the pool
scours the cement paths
when the invisible fingers of the wind suddenly finds itself
deep and flowing through the thick brown hair
of that radiant, tanned woman speaking Spanish with her family,
a pale blue towel wrapped around her shoulders,
her legs crossed as she playfully taps her right foot in the air,
as her yellow flip flop dangles like laughter itself,
like the lucky wind.

Ancient Songs

Talk to me.
Tell me your stories
dream girl, my dream woman.
Tell me only what matters.
Let's fall into bed together
and listen to ancient songs.

In Tibet

A friend explained in an email that
in Tibet you simply cannot say goodbye.
Though you may leave, you are never away from your lovers
because *over there* they have no words
to express parting,
of losing a way of conversing with the world,
how a special brand of fooling around with life just vanishes
as if all our laughter and adventures were only dream images,
vivid and exciting, yet impermanent and ever changing like clouds.
In Tibet, according to the email, we're all just hanging out in the universe
as if life were a magnificent bar, a magical cafe,
everyone continually stopping by for a drink or to tell a good story,
all of us really in search of pick-ups on an endless odyssey of love
in a dream kingdom protected by cosmic unknowing,
an enchanted empire far away, yet so nearby and real,
ringed by protective peaks and immune from these tsunamis of sorrow
that fall with each of our tears.

Happy Box

The floppy soggy cardboard carton
gallops gaily end over end
across the shimmering pasture in early afternoon.
The winter sun warms surprised corn stalk stubs and clumps of grass.
Dark brown trees wooly and willful
on the mountainside seem poised to flower.
The kids and I sing "I Want to Hold Your Hand"
as loud as we can
a carol from a lifetime ago
in the car on Christmas Eve.
Three years further
down the lonesome highway.

Full of Life

Everyone is full of life she said.
I wonder if that's true
at nighttime, with lights out the window, voices from the street.
We seem alive
but do we possess the fire
unquenched or never touched
to still light the world,
even the small closets of our apartment lives,
these unseen corners of our wounded hearts.
Everyone is full of life she said.
Even these countless radiant and broken faces,
these handshakes, caresses, kisses,
high fives, outcries, back slaps, smirks,
these furrowed brows and dances that appear
as I wrestle my dark angel tonight.
Everyone is full of life she said.
And then I thought maybe what she wrote
was hope itself, hope come calling,
surprising, crying my name
in some new way.

A Lover's Words

We should be
looking more
closely
listening
to silence more
finding
in our restlessness
heart song too.

Fireflies

stars on the hazy summer lawn
by my front door
coming home
twinkling low around two cherry trees
that flowered in spring for us.
I step carefully off the path
into the flickering yellow lights
extend my arms like a blind man.
My heart searches helplessly.
I wonder
is this the sacred place
where our love chose
to quietly die.

Last Love Poem

So much love to you,
lavender, boundless and cascading
upon just you, special you there,
now, where you are, where I cannot see or be,
across your splendid face, through your wild and miraculous hair,
into your dazzling eyes and that smile that lit the world for me.
All my wayward love rains down upon you forever dear
showers of that golden childlike love dust
we shared and played upon and laughed about.
Powerful gusts of passion and dreaminess flow out to you
with the beating of my grateful heart,
and wherever and whenever I fall asleep
within this friendly and solitary world,
love will come to you, to special you,
with the closing of my eyes,
always from me
to you, my dark sunflower
always close by
so splendid
yet always so distant

Boyish Questions

Why
does God
let us make
mistakes,
lie, fool ourselves
countless times,
steal, hurt
others, ourselves.
Why
does God
make us
give in
to such terrible trouble?
Why
does God?
Why
does God
let us fall
off a cliff?
Why does
God?
I believe
it's so
we learn
to fall
upwards.

Finally

in the end
when we arrive
where we are
destined to be
we will have
gotten
over
ourselves
finally

Hamburger

We live
on the edge
of our dreams
hanging on
to purple clouds
of our own unknowing.
Hey, maybe it's up there with the moon,
or in the sun tomorrow.
A short round chick
shades and snapping gum
rushes by with a small paper bag.
I'm not going all over this fucking city
with this fucking hamburger.
No angel
ever spoke
more truly.

Firefly Fountain

Laughing children race,
grabbing for magic stars,
fireflies on the lawn
by my front door.
I sit by the low splashing fountain,
guarded by Ray Bans,
imagining how it used to be.

Tickets

Let the great world spirit come to us.
You mean now?
I'm not dressed.

The captain groaned, clamped his eyes shut,
screamed, tore his hair, scratched his blotched face,
tried to wrench himself free of his panicked young men.
With all his power he tried to leap into the churning sea
when they told him his son had shot himself.

The show's totally sold out.
If you want tickets
you have to know somebody.

There's a book in you, you know,
maybe two.

Simply

later
when it's quiet
and all the stars are out
I will reach
for you
in bed
I will reach
for you

Gary Zarr

Up on the Roof

You want a bigger life,
more expansive,
with more sun,
laughter,
instead of this endless searching
in the apartment alone
at 3 in the morning
for the ghost of John Cazale.

You're getting caught up,
way too caught up,
in a life
that's not your own,
in a dream
that's not yours
anymore.

Tom Jobim winks
over there in the corner,
sings Wave in low tones to John Cassavetes,
and the nighttime street lit neon white
crowns their lyric heads
by the window.

You need a bigger life,
more expansive,
with more sun,
more laughter,
the wind
in your face.

The wind
touching every part of you
like a Minoan,
like Laura Nyro
running up on the roof.